The Psychology of Music: A Very Short Introduction

Very Short Introductions available now:

ABOLITIONISM Richard S. Newman
ACCOUNTING Christopher Nobes
ADOLESCENCE Peter K. Smith
ADVERTISING Winston Fletcher
AFRICAN AMERICAN RELIGION
  Eddie S. Glaude Jr
AFRICAN HISTORY John Parker and
  Richard Rathbone
AFRICAN RELIGIONS
  Jacob K. Olupona
AGEING Nancy A. Pachana
AGNOSTICISM Robin Le Poidevin
AGRICULTURE Paul Brassley and
  Richard Soffe
ALEXANDER THE GREAT
  Hugh Bowden
ALGEBRA Peter M. Higgins
AMERICAN CULTURAL HISTORY
  Eric Avila
AMERICAN HISTORY Paul S. Boyer
AMERICAN IMMIGRATION
  David A. Gerber
AMERICAN LEGAL HISTORY
  G. Edward White
AMERICAN POLITICAL HISTORY
  Donald Critchlow
AMERICAN POLITICAL PARTIES
  AND ELECTIONS L. Sandy Maisel
AMERICAN POLITICS
  Richard M. Valelly
THE AMERICAN PRESIDENCY
  Charles O. Jones
THE AMERICAN REVOLUTION
  Robert J. Allison

AMERICAN SLAVERY
  Heather Andrea Williams
THE AMERICAN WEST Stephen Aron
AMERICAN WOMEN'S HISTORY
  Susan Ware
ANAESTHESIA Aidan O'Donnell
ANALYTIC PHILOSOPHY
  Michael Beaney
ANARCHISM Colin Ward
ANCIENT ASSYRIA Karen Radner
ANCIENT EGYPT Ian Shaw
ANCIENT EGYPTIAN ART AND
  ARCHITECTURE Christina Riggs
ANCIENT GREECE Paul Cartledge
THE ANCIENT NEAR EAST
  Amanda H. Podany
ANCIENT PHILOSOPHY Julia Annas
ANCIENT WARFARE
  Harry Sidebottom
ANGELS David Albert Jones
ANGLICANISM Mark Chapman
THE ANGLO-SAXON AGE John Blair
ANIMAL BEHAVIOUR
  Tristram D. Wyatt
THE ANIMAL KINGDOM
  Peter Holland
ANIMAL RIGHTS David DeGrazia
THE ANTARCTIC Klaus Dodds
ANTHROPOCENE Erle C. Ellis
ANTISEMITISM Steven Beller
ANXIETY Daniel Freeman and
  Jason Freeman
APPLIED MATHEMATICS
  Alain Goriely

THE APOCRYPHAL GOSPELS
  Paul Foster
ARCHAEOLOGY Paul Bahn
ARCHITECTURE Andrew Ballantyne
ARISTOCRACY William Doyle
ARISTOTLE Jonathan Barnes
ART HISTORY Dana Arnold
ART THEORY Cynthia Freeland
ARTIFICIAL INTELLIGENCE
  Margaret A. Boden
ASIAN AMERICAN HISTORY
  Madeline Y. Hsu
ASTROBIOLOGY David C. Catling
ASTROPHYSICS James Binney
ATHEISM Julian Baggini
THE ATMOSPHERE Paul I. Palmer
AUGUSTINE Henry Chadwick
AUSTRALIA Kenneth Morgan
AUTISM Uta Frith
AUTOBIOGRAPHY Laura Marcus
THE AVANT GARDE David Cottington
THE AZTECS David Carrasco
BABYLONIA Trevor Bryce
BACTERIA Sebastian G. B. Amyes
BANKING John Goddard and
  John O. S. Wilson
BARTHES Jonathan Culler
THE BEATS David Sterritt
BEAUTY Roger Scruton
BEHAVIOURAL ECONOMICS
  Michelle Baddeley
BESTSELLERS John Sutherland
THE BIBLE John Riches
BIBLICAL ARCHAEOLOGY
  Eric H. Cline
BIG DATA Dawn E. Holmes
BIOGRAPHY Hermione Lee
BLACK HOLES Katherine Blundell
BLOOD Chris Cooper
THE BLUES Elijah Wald
THE BODY Chris Shilling
THE BOOK OF COMMON PRAYER
  Brian Cummings
THE BOOK OF MORMON
  Terryl Givens
BORDERS Alexander C. Diener and
  Joshua Hagen
THE BRAIN Michael O'Shea
BRANDING Robert Jones
THE BRICS Andrew F. Cooper

THE BRITISH CONSTITUTION
  Martin Loughlin
THE BRITISH EMPIRE Ashley Jackson
BRITISH POLITICS Anthony Wright
BUDDHA Michael Carrithers
BUDDHISM Damien Keown
BUDDHIST ETHICS Damien Keown
BYZANTIUM Peter Sarris
CALVINISM Jon Balserak
CANCER Nicholas James
CAPITALISM James Fulcher
CATHOLICISM Gerald O'Collins
CAUSATION Stephen Mumford and
  Rani Lill Anjum
THE CELL Terence Allen and
  Graham Cowling
THE CELTS Barry Cunliffe
CHAOS Leonard Smith
CHEMISTRY Peter Atkins
CHILD PSYCHOLOGY Usha Goswami
CHILDREN'S LITERATURE
  Kimberley Reynolds
CHINESE LITERATURE Sabina Knight
CHOICE THEORY Michael Allingham
CHRISTIAN ART Beth Williamson
CHRISTIAN ETHICS D. Stephen Long
CHRISTIANITY Linda Woodhead
CIRCADIAN RHYTHMS
  Russell Foster and Leon Kreitzman
CITIZENSHIP Richard Bellamy
CIVIL ENGINEERING
  David Muir Wood
CLASSICAL LITERATURE William Allan
CLASSICAL MYTHOLOGY
  Helen Morales
CLASSICS Mary Beard and
  John Henderson
CLAUSEWITZ Michael Howard
CLIMATE Mark Maslin
CLIMATE CHANGE Mark Maslin
CLINICAL PSYCHOLOGY
  Susan Llewelyn and
  Katie Aafjes-van Doorn
COGNITIVE NEUROSCIENCE
  Richard Passingham
THE COLD WAR Robert McMahon
COLONIAL AMERICA Alan Taylor
COLONIAL LATIN AMERICAN
  LITERATURE Rolena Adorno
COMBINATORICS Robin Wilson

COMEDY Matthew Bevis
COMMUNISM Leslie Holmes
COMPARATIVE LITERATURE
    Ben Hutchinson
COMPLEXITY John H. Holland
THE COMPUTER Darrel Ince
COMPUTER SCIENCE
    Subrata Dasgupta
CONFUCIANISM Daniel K. Gardner
THE CONQUISTADORS
    Matthew Restall and
    Felipe Fernández-Armesto
CONSCIENCE Paul Strohm
CONSCIOUSNESS Susan Blackmore
CONTEMPORARY ART
    Julian Stallabrass
CONTEMPORARY FICTION
    Robert Eaglestone
CONTINENTAL PHILOSOPHY
    Simon Critchley
COPERNICUS Owen Gingerich
CORAL REEFS Charles Sheppard
CORPORATE SOCIAL
    RESPONSIBILITY
    Jeremy Moon
CORRUPTION Leslie Holmes
COSMOLOGY Peter Coles
CRIME FICTION Richard Bradford
CRIMINAL JUSTICE Julian V. Roberts
CRIMINOLOGY Tim Newburn
CRITICAL THEORY
    Stephen Eric Bronner
THE CRUSADES Christopher Tyerman
CRYPTOGRAPHY Fred Piper and
    Sean Murphy
CRYSTALLOGRAPHY A. M. Glazer
THE CULTURAL REVOLUTION
    Richard Curt Kraus
DADA AND SURREALISM
    David Hopkins
DANTE Peter Hainsworth and
    David Robey
DARWIN Jonathan Howard
THE DEAD SEA SCROLLS
    Timothy H. Lim
DECOLONIZATION Dane Kennedy
DEMOCRACY Bernard Crick
DEMOGRAPHY Sarah Harper
DEPRESSION Jan Scott and
    Mary Jane Tacchi

DERRIDA Simon Glendinning
DESCARTES Tom Sorell
DESERTS Nick Middleton
DESIGN John Heskett
DEVELOPMENT Ian Goldin
DEVELOPMENTAL BIOLOGY
    Lewis Wolpert
THE DEVIL Darren Oldridge
DIASPORA Kevin Kenny
DICTIONARIES Lynda Mugglestone
DINOSAURS David Norman
DIPLOMACY Joseph M. Siracusa
DOCUMENTARY FILM
    Patricia Aufderheide
DREAMING J. Allan Hobson
DRUGS Les Iversen
DRUIDS Barry Cunliffe
EARLY MUSIC Thomas Forrest Kelly
THE EARTH Martin Redfern
EARTH SYSTEM SCIENCE Tim Lenton
ECONOMICS Partha Dasgupta
EDUCATION Gary Thomas
EGYPTIAN MYTH Geraldine Pinch
EIGHTEENTH-CENTURY
    BRITAIN Paul Langford
THE ELEMENTS Philip Ball
EMOTION Dylan Evans
EMPIRE Stephen Howe
ENGELS Terrell Carver
ENGINEERING David Blockley
THE ENGLISH LANGUAGE
    Simon Horobin
ENGLISH LITERATURE
    Jonathan Bate
THE ENLIGHTENMENT
    John Robertson
ENTREPRENEURSHIP Paul Westhead
    and Mike Wright
ENVIRONMENTAL
    ECONOMICS Stephen Smith
ENVIRONMENTAL LAW
    Elizabeth Fisher
ENVIRONMENTAL POLITICS
    Andrew Dobson
EPICUREANISM Catherine Wilson
EPIDEMIOLOGY Rodolfo Saracci
ETHICS Simon Blackburn
ETHNOMUSICOLOGY Timothy Rice
THE ETRUSCANS Christopher Smith
EUGENICS Philippa Levine

THE EUROPEAN UNION
    Simon Usherwood and John Pinder
EUROPEAN UNION LAW
    Anthony Arnull
EVOLUTION Brian and
    Deborah Charlesworth
EXISTENTIALISM Thomas Flynn
EXPLORATION Stewart A. Weaver
THE EYE Michael Land
FAIRY TALE Marina Warner
FAMILY LAW Jonathan Herring
FASCISM Kevin Passmore
FASHION Rebecca Arnold
FEMINISM Margaret Walters
FILM Michael Wood
FILM MUSIC Kathryn Kalinak
THE FIRST WORLD WAR
    Michael Howard
FOLK MUSIC Mark Slobin
FOOD John Krebs
FORENSIC PSYCHOLOGY
    David Canter
FORENSIC SCIENCE Jim Fraser
FORESTS Jaboury Ghazoul
FOSSILS Keith Thomson
FOUCAULT Gary Gutting
THE FOUNDING FATHERS
    R. B. Bernstein
FRACTALS Kenneth Falconer
FREE SPEECH Nigel Warburton
FREE WILL Thomas Pink
FREEMASONRY Andreas Önnerfors
FRENCH LITERATURE John D. Lyons
THE FRENCH REVOLUTION
    William Doyle
FREUD Anthony Storr
FUNDAMENTALISM Malise Ruthven
FUNGI Nicholas P. Money
THE FUTURE Jennifer M. Gidley
GALAXIES John Gribbin
GALILEO Stillman Drake
GAME THEORY Ken Binmore
GANDHI Bhikhu Parekh
GENES Jonathan Slack
GENIUS Andrew Robinson
GENOMICS John Archibald
GEOGRAPHY John Matthews and
    David Herbert
GEOLOGY Jan Zalasiewicz
GEOPHYSICS William Lowrie

GEOPOLITICS Klaus Dodds
GERMAN LITERATURE Nicholas Boyle
GERMAN PHILOSOPHY
    Andrew Bowie
GLOBAL CATASTROPHES Bill McGuire
GLOBAL ECONOMIC HISTORY
    Robert C. Allen
GLOBALIZATION Manfred Steger
GOD John Bowker
GOETHE Ritchie Robertson
THE GOTHIC Nick Groom
GOVERNANCE Mark Bevir
GRAVITY Timothy Clifton
THE GREAT DEPRESSION AND
    THE NEW DEAL Eric Rauchway
HABERMAS James Gordon Finlayson
THE HABSBURG EMPIRE
    Martyn Rady
HAPPINESS Daniel M. Haybron
THE HARLEM RENAISSANCE
    Cheryl A. Wall
THE HEBREW BIBLE AS
    LITERATURE Tod Linafelt
HEGEL Peter Singer
HEIDEGGER Michael Inwood
THE HELLENISTIC AGE
    Peter Thonemann
HEREDITY John Waller
HERMENEUTICS Jens Zimmermann
HERODOTUS Jennifer T. Roberts
HIEROGLYPHS Penelope Wilson
HINDUISM Kim Knott
HISTORY John H. Arnold
THE HISTORY OF ASTRONOMY
    Michael Hoskin
THE HISTORY OF CHEMISTRY
    William H. Brock
THE HISTORY OF CINEMA
    Geoffrey Nowell-Smith
THE HISTORY OF LIFE
    Michael Benton
THE HISTORY OF MATHEMATICS
    Jacqueline Stedall
THE HISTORY OF MEDICINE
    William Bynum
THE HISTORY OF PHYSICS
    J. L. Heilbron
THE HISTORY OF TIME
    Leofranc Holford-Strevens
HIV AND AIDS Alan Whiteside

HOBBES Richard Tuck
HOLLYWOOD Peter Decherney
THE HOLY ROMAN EMPIRE
    Joachim Whaley
HOME Michael Allen Fox
HORMONES Martin Luck
HUMAN ANATOMY
    Leslie Klenerman
HUMAN EVOLUTION Bernard Wood
HUMAN RIGHTS Andrew Clapham
HUMANISM Stephen Law
HUME A. J. Ayer
HUMOUR Noël Carroll
THE ICE AGE Jamie Woodward
IDEOLOGY Michael Freeden
THE IMMUNE SYSTEM
    Paul Klenerman
INDIAN CINEMA
    Ashish Rajadhyaksha
INDIAN PHILOSOPHY Sue Hamilton
THE INDUSTRIAL REVOLUTION
    Robert C. Allen
INFECTIOUS DISEASE Marta L. Wayne
    and Benjamin M. Bolker
INFINITY Ian Stewart
INFORMATION Luciano Floridi
INNOVATION Mark Dodgson and
    David Gann
INTELLIGENCE Ian J. Deary
INTELLECTUAL PROPERTY
    Siva Vaidhyanathan
INTERNATIONAL LAW
    Vaughan Lowe
INTERNATIONAL MIGRATION
    Khalid Koser
INTERNATIONAL RELATIONS
    Paul Wilkinson
INTERNATIONAL SECURITY
    Christopher S. Browning
IRAN Ali M. Ansari
ISLAM Malise Ruthven
ISLAMIC HISTORY Adam Silverstein
ISOTOPES Rob Ellam
ITALIAN LITERATURE
    Peter Hainsworth and David Robey
JESUS Richard Bauckham
JEWISH HISTORY David N. Myers
JOURNALISM Ian Hargreaves
JUDAISM Norman Solomon
JUNG Anthony Stevens

KABBALAH Joseph Dan
KAFKA Ritchie Robertson
KANT Roger Scruton
KEYNES Robert Skidelsky
KIERKEGAARD Patrick Gardiner
KNOWLEDGE Jennifer Nagel
THE KORAN Michael Cook
LAKES Warwick F. Vincent
LANDSCAPE ARCHITECTURE
    Ian H. Thompson
LANDSCAPES AND
    GEOMORPHOLOGY
    Andrew Goudie and Heather Viles
LANGUAGES Stephen R. Anderson
LATE ANTIQUITY Gillian Clark
LAW Raymond Wacks
THE LAWS OF THERMODYNAMICS
    Peter Atkins
LEADERSHIP Keith Grint
LEARNING Mark Haselgrove
LEIBNIZ Maria Rosa Antognazza
LIBERALISM Michael Freeden
LIGHT Ian Walmsley
LINCOLN Allen C. Guelzo
LINGUISTICS Peter Matthews
LITERARY THEORY Jonathan Culler
LOCKE John Dunn
LOGIC Graham Priest
LOVE Ronald de Sousa
MACHIAVELLI Quentin Skinner
MADNESS Andrew Scull
MAGIC Owen Davies
MAGNA CARTA Nicholas Vincent
MAGNETISM Stephen Blundell
MALTHUS Donald Winch
MAMMALS T. S. Kemp
MANAGEMENT John Hendry
MAO Delia Davin
MARINE BIOLOGY Philip V. Mladenov
THE MARQUIS DE SADE John Phillips
MARTIN LUTHER Scott H. Hendrix
MARTYRDOM Jolyon Mitchell
MARX Peter Singer
MATERIALS Christopher Hall
MATHEMATICS Timothy Gowers
THE MEANING OF LIFE
    Terry Eagleton
MEASUREMENT David Hand
MEDICAL ETHICS Tony Hope
MEDICAL LAW Charles Foster

MEDIEVAL BRITAIN John Gillingham
  and Ralph A. Griffiths
MEDIEVAL LITERATURE
  Elaine Treharne
MEDIEVAL PHILOSOPHY
  John Marenbon
MEMORY Jonathan K. Foster
METAPHYSICS Stephen Mumford
THE MEXICAN REVOLUTION
  Alan Knight
MICHAEL FARADAY
  Frank A. J. L. James
MICROBIOLOGY Nicholas P. Money
MICROECONOMICS Avinash Dixit
MICROSCOPY Terence Allen
THE MIDDLE AGES Miri Rubin
MILITARY JUSTICE Eugene R. Fidell
MILITARY STRATEGY
  Antulio J. Echevarria II
MINERALS David Vaughan
MIRACLES Yujin Nagasawa
MODERN ART David Cottington
MODERN CHINA Rana Mitter
MODERN DRAMA
  Kirsten E. Shepherd-Barr
MODERN FRANCE
  Vanessa R. Schwartz
MODERN INDIA Craig Jeffrey
MODERN IRELAND Senia Pašeta
MODERN ITALY Anna Cento Bull
MODERN JAPAN
  Christopher Goto-Jones
MODERN LATIN AMERICAN
  LITERATURE
  Roberto González Echevarría
MODERN WAR Richard English
MODERNISM Christopher Butler
MOLECULAR BIOLOGY Aysha Divan
  and Janice A. Royds
MOLECULES Philip Ball
MONASTICISM Stephen J. Davis
THE MONGOLS Morris Rossabi
MOONS David A. Rothery
MORMONISM
  Richard Lyman Bushman
MOUNTAINS Martin F. Price
MUHAMMAD Jonathan A. C. Brown
MULTICULTURALISM Ali Rattansi
MULTILINGUALISM John C. Maher
MUSIC Nicholas Cook

MYTH Robert A. Segal
THE NAPOLEONIC WARS
  Mike Rapport
NATIONALISM Steven Grosby
NATIVE AMERICAN LITERATURE
  Sean Teuton
NAVIGATION Jim Bennett
NELSON MANDELA Elleke Boehmer
NEOLIBERALISM Manfred Steger and
  Ravi Roy
NETWORKS Guido Caldarelli and
  Michele Catanzaro
THE NEW TESTAMENT
  Luke Timothy Johnson
THE NEW TESTAMENT AS
  LITERATURE Kyle Keefer
NEWTON Robert Iliffe
NIETZSCHE Michael Tanner
NINETEENTH-CENTURY BRITAIN
  Christopher Harvie and
  H. C. G. Matthew
THE NORMAN CONQUEST
  George Garnett
NORTH AMERICAN INDIANS
  Theda Perdue and
  Michael D. Green
NORTHERN IRELAND
  Marc Mulholland
NOTHING Frank Close
NUCLEAR PHYSICS Frank Close
NUCLEAR POWER Maxwell Irvine
NUCLEAR WEAPONS
  Joseph M. Siracusa
NUMBERS Peter M. Higgins
NUTRITION David A. Bender
OBJECTIVITY Stephen Gaukroger
OCEANS Dorrik Stow
THE OLD TESTAMENT
  Michael D. Coogan
THE ORCHESTRA D. Kern Holoman
ORGANIC CHEMISTRY
  Graham Patrick
ORGANIZED CRIME
  Georgios A. Antonopoulos and
  Georgios Papanicolaou
ORGANIZATIONS Mary Jo Hatch
PAGANISM Owen Davies
PAIN Rob Boddice
THE PALESTINIAN-ISRAELI
  CONFLICT Martin Bunton

PANDEMICS Christian W. McMillen
PARTICLE PHYSICS Frank Close
PAUL E. P. Sanders
PEACE Oliver P. Richmond
PENTECOSTALISM William K. Kay
PERCEPTION Brian Rogers
THE PERIODIC TABLE Eric R. Scerri
PHILOSOPHY Edward Craig
PHILOSOPHY IN THE ISLAMIC
   WORLD Peter Adamson
PHILOSOPHY OF LAW
   Raymond Wacks
PHILOSOPHY OF SCIENCE
   Samir Okasha
PHILOSOPHY OF RELIGION
   Tim Bayne
PHOTOGRAPHY Steve Edwards
PHYSICAL CHEMISTRY Peter Atkins
PILGRIMAGE Ian Reader
PLAGUE Paul Slack
PLANETS David A. Rothery
PLANTS Timothy Walker
PLATE TECTONICS Peter Molnar
PLATO Julia Annas
POLITICAL PHILOSOPHY
   David Miller
POLITICS Kenneth Minogue
POPULISM Cas Mudde and
   Cristóbal Rovira Kaltwasser
POSTCOLONIALISM Robert Young
POSTMODERNISM Christopher Butler
POSTSTRUCTURALISM
   Catherine Belsey
POVERTY Philip N. Jefferson
PREHISTORY Chris Gosden
PRESOCRATIC PHILOSOPHY
   Catherine Osborne
PRIVACY Raymond Wacks
PROBABILITY John Haigh
PROGRESSIVISM Walter Nugent
PROJECTS Andrew Davies
PROTESTANTISM Mark A. Noll
PSYCHIATRY Tom Burns
PSYCHOANALYSIS Daniel Pick
PSYCHOLOGY Gillian Butler and
   Freda McManus
PSYCHOLOGY OF MUSIC
   Elizabeth Hellmuth Margulis
PSYCHOTHERAPY Tom Burns and
   Eva Burns-Lundgren

PUBLIC ADMINISTRATION
   Stella Z. Theodoulou and Ravi K. Roy
PUBLIC HEALTH Virginia Berridge
PURITANISM Francis J. Bremer
THE QUAKERS Pink Dandelion
QUANTUM THEORY
   John Polkinghorne
RACISM Ali Rattansi
RADIOACTIVITY Claudio Tuniz
RASTAFARI Ennis B. Edmonds
THE REAGAN REVOLUTION Gil Troy
REALITY Jan Westerhoff
THE REFORMATION Peter Marshall
RELATIVITY Russell Stannard
RELIGION IN AMERICA Timothy Beal
THE RENAISSANCE Jerry Brotton
RENAISSANCE ART
   Geraldine A. Johnson
REVOLUTIONS Jack A. Goldstone
RHETORIC Richard Toye
RISK Baruch Fischhoff and
   John Kadvany
RITUAL Barry Stephenson
RIVERS Nick Middleton
ROBOTICS Alan Winfield
ROCKS Jan Zalasiewicz
ROMAN BRITAIN Peter Salway
THE ROMAN EMPIRE
   Christopher Kelly
THE ROMAN REPUBLIC
   David M. Gwynn
ROMANTICISM Michael Ferber
ROUSSEAU Robert Wokler
RUSSELL A. C. Grayling
RUSSIAN HISTORY Geoffrey Hosking
RUSSIAN LITERATURE Catriona Kelly
THE RUSSIAN REVOLUTION
   S. A. Smith
THE SAINTS Simon Yarrow
SAVANNAS Peter A. Furley
SCHIZOPHRENIA Chris Frith and
   Eve Johnstone
SCHOPENHAUER
   Christopher Janaway
SCIENCE AND RELIGION
   Thomas Dixon
SCIENCE FICTION David Seed
THE SCIENTIFIC REVOLUTION
   Lawrence M. Principe
SCOTLAND Rab Houston

SEXUAL SELECTION Marlene Zuk and
    Leigh W. Simmons
SEXUALITY Véronique Mottier
SHAKESPEARE'S COMEDIES
    Bart van Es
SHAKESPEARE'S SONNETS AND
    POEMS Jonathan F. S. Post
SHAKESPEARE'S TRAGEDIES
    Stanley Wells
SIKHISM Eleanor Nesbitt
THE SILK ROAD James A. Millward
SLANG Jonathon Green
SLEEP Steven W. Lockley and
    Russell G. Foster
SOCIAL AND CULTURAL
    ANTHROPOLOGY
    John Monaghan and Peter Just
SOCIAL PSYCHOLOGY Richard J. Crisp
SOCIAL WORK Sally Holland and
    Jonathan Scourfield
SOCIALISM Michael Newman
SOCIOLINGUISTICS John Edwards
SOCIOLOGY Steve Bruce
SOCRATES C. C. W. Taylor
SOUND Mike Goldsmith
THE SOVIET UNION Stephen Lovell
THE SPANISH CIVIL WAR
    Helen Graham
SPANISH LITERATURE Jo Labanyi
SPINOZA Roger Scruton
SPIRITUALITY Philip Sheldrake
SPORT Mike Cronin
STARS Andrew King
STATISTICS David J. Hand
STEM CELLS Jonathan Slack
STOICISM Brad Inwood
STRUCTURAL ENGINEERING
    David Blockley
STUART BRITAIN John Morrill
SUPERCONDUCTIVITY
    Stephen Blundell
SYMMETRY Ian Stewart
SYNTHETIC BIOLOGY Jamie A. Davies
TAXATION Stephen Smith
TEETH Peter S. Ungar
TELESCOPES Geoff Cottrell
TERRORISM Charles Townshend
THEATRE Marvin Carlson
THEOLOGY David F. Ford

THINKING AND REASONING
    Jonathan St. B. T. Evans
THOMAS AQUINAS Fergus Kerr
THOUGHT Tim Bayne
TIBETAN BUDDHISM
    Matthew T. Kapstein
TOCQUEVILLE Harvey C. Mansfield
TRAGEDY Adrian Poole
TRANSLATION Matthew Reynolds
THE TROJAN WAR Eric H. Cline
TRUST Katherine Hawley
THE TUDORS John Guy
TWENTIETH-CENTURY BRITAIN
    Kenneth O. Morgan
THE UNITED NATIONS
    Jussi M. Hanhimäki
THE U.S. CONGRESS Donald A. Ritchie
THE U.S. CONSTITUTION
    David J. Bodenhamer
THE U.S. SUPREME COURT
    Linda Greenhouse
UTILITARIANISM
    Katarzyna de Lazari-Radek and
    Peter Singer
UNIVERSITIES AND COLLEGES
    David Palfreyman and Paul Temple
UTOPIANISM Lyman Tower Sargent
VETERINARY SCIENCE James Yeates
THE VIKINGS Julian Richards
VIRUSES Dorothy H. Crawford
VOLTAIRE Nicholas Cronk
WAR AND TECHNOLOGY
    Alex Roland
WATER John Finney
WEATHER Storm Dunlop
THE WELFARE STATE David Garland
WILLIAM SHAKESPEARE
    Stanley Wells
WITCHCRAFT Malcolm Gaskill
WITTGENSTEIN A. C. Grayling
WORK Stephen Fineman
WORLD MUSIC Philip Bohlman
THE WORLD TRADE
    ORGANIZATION Amrita Narlikar
WORLD WAR II
    Gerhard L. Weinberg
WRITING AND SCRIPT
    Andrew Robinson
ZIONISM Michael Stanislawski

Available soon:

MODERN ARCHITECTURE
Adam Sharr
ADAM SMITH Christopher J. Berry

BIOMETRICS Michael Fairhurst
GLACIATION David J. A. Evans
AFRICAN POLITICS Ian Taylor

For more information visit our website
www.oup.com/vsi/

Elizabeth Hellmuth Margulis

THE PSYCHOLOGY OF MUSIC

A Very Short Introduction

OXFORD
UNIVERSITY PRESS

OXFORD
UNIVERSITY PRESS

Oxford University Press is a department of the University of Oxford.
It furthers the University's objective of excellence in research, scholarship,
and education by publishing worldwide. Oxford is a registered trade mark of
Oxford University Press in the UK and certain other countries.

Published in the United States of America by Oxford University Press
198 Madison Avenue, New York, NY 10016, United States of America.

© Oxford University Press 2019

Library of Congress Cataloging-in-Publication Data

Names: Margulis, Elizabeth Hellmuth, author.
Title: The Psychology of music : a very short introduction /
Elizabeth Hellmuth Margulis.
Description: Oxford ; New York : Oxford University Press, 2018. | Series:
Very short introductions | Includes bibliographical references and index.
Identifiers: LCCN 2018010769 (print) | LCCN 2018011320 (ebook) |
ISBN 9780190640163 (online component) |
ISBN 9780190640170 (updf) | ISBN 9780190640187 (epub) |
ISBN 9780190640156 (pbk. : alk. paper)
Subjects: LCSH: Music—Psychological aspects.
Classification: LCC ML3830 (ebook) | LCC ML3830 .M29 2018 (print) |
DDC 781.1/1—dc23
LC record available at https://lccn.loc.gov/2018010769

Printed by Integrated Books International, United States of America
on acid-free paper

To Nikolai, Hugo, and Alexander, who are also,
for the moment, very short, and for Martin,
whose patience never is

Contents

List of illustrations xvii

Acknowledgments xix

1 The art and science of music psychology 1

2 The biological origins of music 20

3 Music as language 34

4 Listening in time 49

5 The psychology of music performance 63

6 Human musicality 79

7 The appetite for music 95

8 The future 109

References 123

Further reading 131

Index 133

List of illustrations

1. Carl Seashore's tonoscope **7**
   "A voice tonoscope," C. Seashore, *Iowa State Psychology* III (1902)

2. Schematic of the research process in music psychology **15**
   Author's collection

3. Child undergoing an EEG test **17**
   Author's collection

4. Spectrograms of a person singing and speaking "Twinkle, Twinkle, Little Star" **46**
   Author's collection

5. Auditory stream segregation **56**
   A. S. Bregman and P. A. Ahad, "Demonstrations of Auditory Stream Analysis: The Perceptual Organization of Sound" (1996)

6. Tempo fluctuations in performances of a Chopin étude **67**
   Adapted from L. H. Shaffer, "Timing in Solo and Duet Piano Performances," *Quarterly Journal of Experimental Psychology Section A: Human Experimental Psychology* 36 (1984)

7. Tone profile charting goodness-of-fit ratings **81**
   Adapted from Carol L. Krumhansl and Edward J. Kessler, "Tracing the Dynamic Changes in Perceived Tonal Organization in a Spatial Representation of Musical Keys," *Psychological Review* 89 (1982)

8. A child listening to *Peter and the Wolf* **97**
   Author's collection

9. Curve reflecting the impact of familiarity on preference for a song **104**
   Adapted from W. Wundt, *Grundzüge der physiologischen Psychologie* (1880)

10. Shimon, the marimba-playing robot **114**
    Gil Weinberg

Acknowledgments

Although any errors in the final version are my own, I am grateful to Robert Gjerdingen, Erin Hannon, Daniel Müllensiefen, Carmel Raz, and Renee Timmers for reading portions of the manuscript in early stages and providing helpful feedback. Martin Miller and Theodore Hellmuth gave invaluable commentary on a complete draft. Students in my Honors Colloquium on Music and the Mind at the University of Arkansas over the years helped shape the book's content and focus. A sabbatical from the University of Arkansas enabled me to finish the volume.

Chapter 1
The art and science of music psychology

Music can seem to be the human behavior that is least susceptible to explanation. People all over the world make music—the average American listens to it for four hours a day—yet we are generally not very good at talking about it. This resistance to verbal description has led some philosophers to suggest that music is simply ineffable. "Writing about music," goes one quotation that has been attributed to everyone from Frank Zappa to Thelonious Monk, "is like dancing about architecture."

Yet this difficulty has not stopped generation after generation from using diverse modes of thought to try to make sense of music. Since at least the age of Pythagoras, people have attempted to understand musical structures in terms of mathematics. Musicologists and ethnomusicologists, alternatively, think about music as a product of human history and culture.

Music psychology offers a different framework. It views music as a product of the human mind. One powerful advantage of this perspective is that psychology has developed a clever set of tools to study cognitive processes implicitly, without requiring people to explicitly report on them. Even if a person cannot describe her musical experience in words, psychologists can use neuroimaging or reaction times on a behavioral task to infer the mental processes that made that experience possible.

The psychology of music draws not just on the techniques of behavioral research, but also on the broader collection of approaches known collectively as cognitive science. The cognitive science of music integrates ideas from philosophy, music theory, experimental psychology, neuroscience, anthropology, and computer modeling to answer the big (and little) questions about music's role in human lives. For example, a philosopher might theorize about the phenomenology of musical experience—characterizing what it feels like to listen to music—and this theory might inspire behavioral tests. A music theorist might identify a pattern that appears in thousands of songs. A neuroscientist might investigate responses to this pattern.

Despite this interdisciplinary and collaborative spirit, applying scientific methodologies to the study of music—a humanistic topic, in a typical course catalogue—risks accusations of reductionism, the suspicion that a complex topic is being examined in overly simplistic ways. For example, participants in many studies on the psychology of music are college undergraduates in North America, Europe, or Australia. In standard music psychology studies, participants respond to excerpts of Western tonal music—the kind written in major and minor keys, that you might hear on the radio or at a concert hall in London or Chicago. If studies like these are taken as the sole evidence of universal musical processes, they might fail to acknowledge the profound role culture plays in human perception.

The art of music psychology is to bring rigorous scientific methodologies to questions about the human musical capacity, while applying sophisticated humanistic approaches to framing and interpreting the science. By combining these techniques, music psychology can address questions such as:

- What does it mean to be musical?
- Are some people more musical than others, and if so, why? Can nonhuman animals be musical?

- What aspects of musicality arise from biology, and what aspects from culture?
- How can musical training or experience affect other spheres of life, ranging from language acquisition to memory to health?
- Why do people like music so much? What motivates them to listen to or play it? Why do different people like different music?
- How does music make people feel things?
- In what ways does music function similarly to or differently from language?
- What makes some performances brilliant and others, not so much?
- How are musical skills and tastes acquired over the lifespan, from infancy to old age?
- Why does some music make people want to move—or dance?

Many of these questions have been asked for at least as long as we have written records. To understand contemporary perspectives on them, it helps to consider how they emerged across the course of history.

The history of thinking about music and the mind

As far back as the sixth century BCE, philosophers puzzled over why certain pairs of notes seem to sound good together—or consonant—and others do not. According to legend, Pythagoras discovered in a blacksmith shop that the weights of hammers that produce consonant intervals when striking iron tend to relate to one another by simple integer ratios such as 2:1 or 3:2 (even though this actually holds true for the length of vibrating strings, not for the weights of vibrating metal objects). This discovery seemed to imply that musical perceptions were rooted in a fundamental mathematical truth, understood at the time to echo a "harmony of the spheres" emitted by the orbits of celestial objects. By linking perceived consonance with divinely ordained numeric relationships, this viewpoint presented an appealingly orderly stance: perhaps musical experience could be understood by studying the pure domain of mathematics, rather than the messy domain of human beings. When the Greek philosopher Aristoxenus, in the fourth century BCE, adopted a more empirical approach, shifting the focus from numeric relationships to human sensory and perception systems, his work largely failed to gain traction.

The seduction of factoring people out of the equation when studying music is hardly relegated to ancient Greece. People disagree about what music sounds good—they even disagree about what counts as music. Bypassing their opinions and perceptions makes for much simpler subject matter. Even into the twenty-first century, some music theorists conceptualized music as a collection of abstract structures, amenable to analysis independent of the humans who create or listen to them. One fundamental contribution of the psychology of music is to place human music makers and listeners at the center of research questions on this topic.

The scientific revolution of the sixteenth century provided the first significant cracks in the rationalist perspective. Astronomers discovered that the moon, sun, and planets did not trace circular orbits around the earth, puncturing the philosophical underpinnings of the music of the spheres. Vincenzo Galilei showed that the relationship between simple integer ratios and perceived consonance held only for certain materials under certain circumstances—it worked for the length of strings that sounded good when plucked together, for example, but not for the volume of bells that sounded good when rung together. By 1600, Francis Bacon was talking about music in terms of the very human process of communicating emotion, rather than in terms of the earthly manifestation of divine proportions. René Descartes, shortly thereafter, was considering the notion that simple ratios were more pleasing because the sensory system could process them more effectively than complex ones.

Yet even in shifting the focus to human listeners, scholars were not immune to the appeal of reductionism. Some of the most influential musical thinkers of the eighteenth and nineteenth centuries, including Jean-Philippe Rameau and Hugo Riemann, still managed to depict musical structures as arising inevitably from a set of laws—laws newly cast as perceptual rather than acoustic. They asserted primacy for the Western mode of organizing pitch, attributing it to the interaction of the physics of sound and the physiological characteristics of the ear. The title of Hermann Helmholtz's 1863 treatise encapsulates the aspirations of researchers at this time: *On the Sensations of Tone as a Physiological Basis for the Theory of Music.*

The scientists who followed Helmholtz were entranced by the notion of applying methodological rigor to a topic as amorphous as music. To achieve this rigor, they conducted experiments using simplified, artificial stimuli (disdainfully referred to by some contemporary researchers as "beeps and boops") presented one at a time, without context. Unsurprisingly, perhaps, this research did not capture the imagination of musicians, and it largely failed to offer insights relevant to broader musical practices.

Exceptions to this trend include work around the turn of the twentieth century by Richard Wallanschek, who used neurology to examine high-level musical topics such as meter—the organization of sounds in time—and program notes, the descriptions that concert halls often provide to classical concertgoers. Wallanschek argued that program notes were a waste of effort because intellectual information and emotional information were processed in different channels of the brain, and no amount of rational analysis could affect a person's fundamentally emotional experience of a piece—a supposition roundly contradicted by subsequent research. More troublingly and equally falsely, Wallanschek also appealed to neurology to elucidate what he viewed as the superiority of European to African music.

These two opposing trends in early-twentieth-century research—toward rigorously investigating low-level phenomena with little musical relevance, on the one hand, and investigating high-level phenomena with little cultural awareness, on the other—establish a set of twin dangers around which the psychology of music still aims to navigate today. Studies that avoid the complexities of everyday music and instead use carefully controlled, synthetic stimuli can fail to shed light on real-world musical behaviors, but studies that target actual musical experiences—if not appropriately framed and interpreted with humanistic sophistication—can seem misleadingly to confer the stamp of science on cultural misassumptions.

The early-twentieth-century work of psychologist Carl Seashore—despite its creativity and substantial influence—exemplifies both these dangers. Seashore devised tests to assess people's individual musical potential. These tests involved such tasks as listening to two tones and judging which was higher or listening to three clicks and deciding whether a longer span of time separated the first or second pair. They were administered in 1922 to all children in the fifth and sixth grades in the Des Moines, Iowa, public schools, and praised by *Scientific American* as "well-nigh flawless." Seashore articulated an optimistic vision, in which his tests might allow farm boys with latent musical talent to receive training on an instrument and the chance to connect to a broader musical world. But the tests were implemented with a darker, winnowing purpose—the *Scientific American* article touts the "enormous economic importance" of the tests, owing to "the amount of money which is wasted upon children in the United States who can never become musicians." If a child did not pass, in other words, why waste time and money trying to squeeze performances out of a musical dunce?

Seashore's project used simplified stimuli like tones and clicks, presented in isolation, and interpreted responses to them as indicative of a high-level cultural phenomenon musical aptitude. The societal power of science gave the study the authoritative

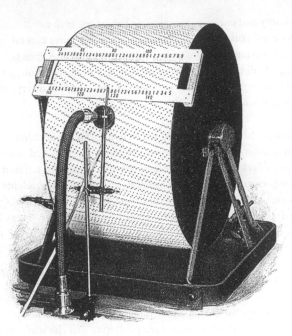

1. Carl Seashore devised the tonoscope to record and measure the acoustic characteristics of sung pitches, one component of his battery of tests designed to identify "musical talent."

force to support an otherwise hazy and little-examined assumption—in this case, the assumption that musical aptitude is innate and unevenly distributed among the population. It could then be used to guide real-world decisions on questions such as who should have access to music education.

Work in the psychology of music typically depends on taking a high-level, interesting concept (for example, musical aptitude, or musical memory, or emotional response) and—in a process referred to as operationalizing—identifying a measurable behavior that can be taken to represent it. Therein lies the art. Slipping back and forth between broad humanistic concepts such as musicality and concrete measurable behaviors, such as performance on a pitch discrimination task, requires careful interpretive logic, and, as with Seashore, it can sometimes go wrong. Of all the phenomena in the history of the psychology of music, perhaps none better exemplifies the danger of interpretive slippage than the notion of the Mozart effect.

It started with a 1993 study in which college students either listened to ten minutes of a sonata by Mozart, or listened to ten minutes of relaxation instructions, or sat in silence for ten minutes before performing a spatial reasoning task. When the students performed the task within ten to fifteen minutes after listening to Mozart, their spatial reasoning scores were higher than if they had relaxed or sat in silence.

In a climate of parental anxiety about children's intelligence and widespread notions that artists and musicians in the Western canon possessed special genius, the details of the study's design got lost. In the mind of the general public, science had just proved that Mozart made children smarter—despite that the study had not used children and had not measured general intelligence, and, as the authors carefully noted, that the effect of listening to Mozart disappeared after fifteen minutes.

Eager to reap these benefits, the governor of Georgia in 1998 arranged for classical music CDs to be distributed to all parents of newborns in the state, and the Florida legislature proposed that state-funded day-care centers be required to play classical music for their charges every day. These well-intentioned initiatives were based on interpretive slippage, where short-term improvements on a spatial reasoning task were taken to represent general intelligence and where college students were taken to represent toddlers. How could this happen?

For one thing, in an effort to highlight the relevance of scientific findings, the media sometimes generalize results in a way that encourages more interest but does not carefully acknowledge interpretive limits. For another, people tend to understand new findings in terms of existing cultural narratives. Well before the Mozart study, a prevalent cultural narrative outlined the supposed intellectual superiority of classical music, in general, and its most renowned composers, in particular. Within this framework, it was easy to believe that passive exposure to Mozart's music might have ennobling effects.

From a scientific standpoint, however, the original study could not demonstrate anything about the comparative efficacy of Mozart or classical music compared to other composers and other traditions because the comparison conditions involved sitting in silence or listening to relaxation instructions. Only by comparing the effect of listening to Mozart with the effect of listening to Beethoven or Ravi Shankar or the Beatles could any special benefit of this particular music, rather than of music in general, be established. In fact, when studies like these were eventually run, it became clear that the same short-term benefit could be achieved by any music, so long as it was moderately upbeat and engaging. The boost in cognitive performance could be attributed to arousal, not to Mozart. Walking briskly on a treadmill produces the same benefit. When people are brought into a stimulated and focused state they perform better on tests.

Yet despite these subsequent findings, and despite failures to replicate the original study, aisles and aisles of plastic baby toys still feature buttons that deploy Mozart tunes when pressed. Baby Mozart, in fact, is a trademarked brand. It can take decades of scientists and journalists and musicians talking and writing and playing to reshape dominant cultural narratives. Increasing the pace of general societal understanding would require broader engagement with the interpretive logic used to move back and forth between data and interpretation. The psychology of music is uniquely well poised to advance this engagement because scholars in this area have already been participating in a form of translation since the early 1980s: between the humanities and the sciences. By learning how to communicate across disciplinary boundaries, they have paved the way for better communication with the music-making and music-listening public at large.

Contemporary approaches to music and the mind

In the early twentieth century, experimental psychology was dazzled by the potential of studying behavior. Inspired by Pavlov and his salivating dogs, Harvard psychologist B. F. Skinner sought to bracket off the mind as a black box, not amenable to scientific study, and understand humans instead by rigorously measuring their behavior. But by the 1950s, the disciplines of computer science and neuroscience had begun to emerge in parallel. They introduced a set of methods for peering inside black boxes that perform computations, both computers and brains. As people strived to answer big questions about human thought, a new paradigm linking psychology, computer science, anthropology, linguistics, and neuroscience came to be known as cognitive science.

One of the big questions that united these fields concerned the nature of human language. How does it work and how do babies learn it so quickly over their first few years of life? People engaged in research about the human capacity for language came to view music as an interesting comparison case. Like language, music consists of the complex patterning of individual sound elements. Like language, music varies across human cultures. Like language, music occurs dynamically in time, and it is capable of being notated. And arguably, like language, music seems to be unique to humans.

Contemporary work in the psychology of music owes much to the psychology of language, adopting many of its theories and methods. Various approaches have come to form the core of this new field of study: computer modeling, corpus studies, behavioral research, cognitive neuroscience methods, clinical approaches, and qualitative approaches.

Computer modeling

One way to find out how a human might perform a task is to program a computer to do it. How do people compose music, for example? In the 1980s, researchers tackled this question by trying to get a computer to write music in the style of composers such as Bach and Mozart. A recent project at Google titled *Magenta* has taken on an even more ambitious goal: attempting to harness the power of machine learning to elicit compelling original music from computers. These kinds of projects rely on the notion that the brain, like a computer, can be productively conceptualized as an information-processing machine. By identifying the strategies a computer must use to produce engaging music, these endeavors provide initial hypotheses for how the brain might accomplish the same task.

Scientists have also harnessed computer modeling to address questions such as: How do people decide which beats to clap on when they're listening to music? How do performers make expressive decisions, such as which notes to linger on, which to shorten, which to play louder, and which to introduce after a subtle delay? How do listeners decide which notes sound tense and which sound relaxed in a particular piece? These questions can be challenging to tackle. Programming a computer to model some aspect of the topic under consideration—no matter how inadequate the model might ultimately prove—can help establish a tractable place to start. For example, in thinking about how people can tap along to the beat so easily, one could form an initial hypothesis that they simply tap whenever the loudness of the music exceeds a certain threshold. By programming a computer with this strategy and observing the way it taps or mis-taps to various songs, the limitations of this theory can be exposed. Adding new strategies to the model—tapping when the lowest note dips below a certain limit or building in a function that favors tapping across regularly spaced intervals—can refine existing theories about how humans track the musical beat. Behavioral researchers can then set up studies that systematically vary the loudness and pitch height in musical examples and track the changes in how people tap to these excerpts. In this way, computer modeling and experimental psychology can partner to advance the understanding of human musical processing.

Corpus studies

Increased digitization has made it possible to identify patterns in huge sets of data that are too large to investigate by hand. It now takes mere minutes to count the number of Bs or Cs or F-sharps in the Haydn string quartets, or in Japanese nineteenth-century popular songs, and to compare these distributions. It is similarly straightforward to tally all the timing and loudness modifications made by singers and pianists in dozens of recordings of a particular Schubert song.

The kind of data represented by notated music and recorded performance is extensive, and allows researchers to ask questions fundamental to music psychology. For example, people often slow down at the end of spoken phrases. By measuring timing patterns in recorded performances, researchers discovered that people also slow down at the end of musical phrases, revealing more about the relationship between language and music. Moreover, by looking at how these timing patterns vary as a function of time and place, corpus studies can shed light on the degree to which such patterns are influenced by culture rather than by biology. Best of all, these studies can be done with a computer and a little programming knowledge—there is no need to recruit participants or set up a lab. Many corpus studies, however, depend on databases that encode musical notation or audio in special ways to make them easy to query—the development of these databases is often the most resource-intensive part of this kind of work. Choices about what aspects of the music get represented in the database influence what kinds of insight can be gained from studying it.

Behavioral research

Many questions in the psychology of music are answerable only by studying behavior under controlled conditions. Behavior, in this context, can designate any kind of measurable response made by a person—reaction time when performing a task, or toe taps, or answers to particular questions. For example, researchers might want to know whether it is easier to remember certain kinds of melodic patterns. Ideally, they would like to know whether this memory boost extends to all people, but since it is not feasible to test everyone, they select a random sample and use statistics to determine whether their findings are likely to generalize to the larger population. But many studies in music psychology use undergraduates at universities in the West as participants—hardly a random sample of people in the world. Rather than illuminating how all humans hear music these studies might more aptly be thought to examine how humans with a particular cultural background do.

During an experimental session, participants may be ushered one at a time into a soundproof booth in a laboratory and played stimuli consisting of different musical patterns over headphones. Then, they may be played pairs of patterns and asked which they heard in the first part of the experiment. If they provide more correct responses for a particular type of pattern, statistical tools can assess the chances that this difference reflects a real effect present in the larger population (people really remember this pattern more easily) or occurred by chance (it is actually equally easy to remember both patterns, but random error led to the appearance of a difference).

One important challenge for this type of research is ecological validity—to what extent are the cognitive processes people use to make sense of simplified stimuli in a laboratory environment representative of the processes they use to make sense of rich, socially embedded musical experiences in the real world? Although this challenge characterizes much work in the social sciences, it is particularly relevant to research that tackles a complex cultural behavior like music.

Big, humanistic questions often motivate research in the psychology of music: What drives musical enjoyment? Why are humans musical? Yet people designing experiments must identify ways to operationalize these concepts—ways to test and measure them discretely and tractably. This is the first juncture at which a substantial amount of art enters into the science. Experiments that operationalize important concepts in misleading ways can result in science that might look robust at first glance but ultimately prove unsatisfactory. Carl Seashore, for example, wanted to understand the musical potential of children, but he operationalized it using things like performance on a tone discrimination task. Getting children to identify which of two notes 1/108th of a tone apart is higher makes for good quantitative data but hardly seems like a useful measure of musical potential.

Figure 2 depicts the way behavioral research moves between quantitative and qualitative reasoning. First, big questions must be restated in terms of the interaction of measurable variables—a process that requires substantial humanistic insight. Once this funneling has been accomplished, well-established methods can be applied to collect data, measure the results, and specify their likely relationship to the larger population of whom the experiment's participants form a sample. All of this can be conceptualized as taking place within the box at the center of Figure 2. But in the final stage of research, these findings must be interpreted and connected to the larger questions that motivated the study in the first place. Here again lies the need for insight, and the danger for misrepresentation—for example interpreting a study of college students as evidence that Mozart increases the long-term intelligence of babies.

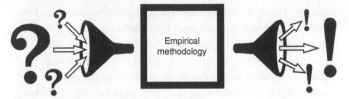

Motivating questions   Empirical methodology   Interpretation

2. Researchers start with motivating questions, often concerning big topics such as emotion or memory. They devise concrete ways of measuring these phenomena behaviorally. Once performance on these tasks has been recorded, they must interpret how the specific findings relate to the broader topic of interest. Especially in the case of research on a cultural phenomenon like music, they must pay careful attention to whether the measured behavior serves as an adequate proxy for the broader topic.

It is almost impossible to satisfactorily operationalize big concepts like emotional experience or musical potential into measurable variables in just one way within just one study. Progress in the psychology of music occurs incrementally across dozens and dozens of projects. Often, limitations in one experiment can be addressed by running a new experiment that controls for a potential confound (another variable that might have been influencing the results) or operationalizes the topic in a new and more powerful way. This potential for progress across multiple studies helps the psychology of music drive toward deeper and deeper insight as a field, even though each individual study might contribute only a limited view.

Because people are often unreliable reporters of their cognitive processes, and because they generally lack direct access to the cognitive processes that underlie their beliefs, experiences, and actions, psychologists have developed a host of clever ways of measuring them implicitly, without relying on direct questions. For example, instead of asking participants how they feel about something, psychologists might measure their reaction time, or respiration rate, or some other indirect indicator of emotional response. This capacity for identifying implicit measures makes experimental psychology an especially useful approach for understanding musical experience. Because people are often unaccustomed or unable to report verbally on their musical experiences, sometimes going so far as to characterize them as fundamentally ineffable or incapable of being described in words, implicit methods that bypass the need for verbal report have special power to illuminate musical experience.

Cognitive neuroscience methods

In addition to inferring aspects of cognitive processing from behavior, researchers in the twenty-first century can use a variety of methods to infer cognitive processing from studying the brain. The cognitive neuroscience techniques used most commonly in the psychology of music are EEG and fMRI.

EEG relies on electrodes placed along the scalp to measure changes in electrical potential, from which neural activity can be inferred. EEG allows the time-course of neural response to be precisely measured. Since music takes place in time, and researchers often want to know what kind of response one particular note might elicit in contrast to another particular note, EEG's capacity to pinpoint responses to individual moments is particularly useful. Its spatial resolution, however, is poor. Complex patterns of neural activity within the three-dimensional structure of the brain sum to influence the recordings of particular electrodes placed on the scalp, making it difficult to identify the exact place where each component originated.

Neuroimaging, however, including fMRI, can provide excellent evidence about the location of neural activity. The trade-off involves poorer temporal resolution, making it less useful for tracking the moment-by-moment perceptual changes as the music progresses. Neuroimaging produces those familiar pictures of the brain within which areas of activity are represented by

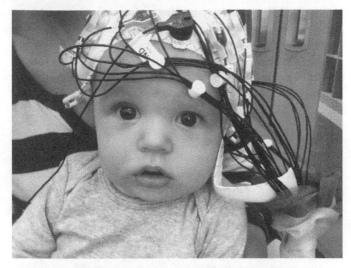

3. EEG caps affix electrodes to the scalp, allowing researchers to measure changes in electrical potential. EEG can be especially useful for inferring neural activity in people who cannot report verbally on their experience, such as this five-month-old infant.

colorful blotches. With fMRI, researchers can ask questions like: Do music and speech rely on the same neural circuitry? Do people engage motor regions when they listen passively to music? Do people with musical training process speech differently than people without it?

Neuroscientific approaches influence the public imagination disproportionately in comparison to other approaches. Studies have shown that people, when provided psychological explanations of varying quality, were able to accurately rate the logic—identifying good arguments as good and bad arguments as bad—until parentheticals alluding to brain regions were added (for example, "as shown by activity in the amygdala"). When bad arguments included allusions to neuroscience, people tended to think the argument was more logically sound.

Neuroimaging's persuasive power makes it an important tool, but also raises the possibility of misinterpretation and overconfidence in the research's assumptions. It is especially important to rigorously evaluate the theory underlying cognitive neuroscience studies of music to ensure that they illuminate rather than misrepresent the rich cultural practice of music.

Clinical approaches

Sometimes it is easiest to learn about human musical processing by studying what goes awry when it is impaired. Clinical studies can look at people with brain damage, for example, and link the injured areas with observed musical deficits to draw conclusions about what capacities depend on what brain regions. Some clinical studies focus on particular conditions, such as the developmental disorder Williams syndrome, that are typically associated with relatively high degrees of musicality.

Clinical approaches can also study music as an intervention, examining the ways that playing, studying, or listening to music can improve health, or the way a particular variety of singing therapy can assist people with aphasia (impaired language following stroke or other brain injury) in learning to speak again. Documentary films such as *Alive Inside* (2014) chronicle the impact music can have on patients with dementia. Clinical research applies rigorous methods to uncovering the most effective therapeutic uses of music.

Qualitative approaches

Some aspects of musical processing are best studied qualitatively, with interviews and surveys and observation. MIT music professor Jeanne Bamberger, for example, laid the foundation for contemporary work in the developmental psychology of music by giving children Montessori bells and asking them to draw representations of what they heard and played. By paging through dozens and dozens of responses, she was able to make inferences about the kinds of musical representation children tended to possess at different ages. Swedish psychologist Alf Gabrielsson interviewed hundreds of people about their peak experiences of music—their most intense and emotional musical moments—and combed through them to identify commonalities.

This kind of close observation can yield theories and hypotheses that subsequent studies can investigate quantitatively. Because musical behaviors are so complex and so various, they can require years of qualitative study before any quantitative approach is possible.

Chapter 2
The biological origins of music

Flutes made of animal bones with perforated finger holes appear in the archaeological record tens of thousands of years ago. Vocal and instrumental music exists in all known human cultures. Music's age and ubiquity seem to argue that its origins are biological. But the diversity of musical practices around the world seems to argue instead that its origins are cultural. This diversity extends to the very notion of what constitutes music: the Blackfoot term *saapup* encompasses singing, dancing, and ceremony, without carving out a separate concept for the purely acoustic. Other languages, including Thai and Sanskrit, have a single word that denotes both music and dance, while still others have separate words for singing and instrumental music but no overarching category that combines them. As an entry point to the debate about music and biology, it can be useful to identify what musical features tend to be shared across cultures. One fascinating—and paradoxical—shared characteristic is a tendency for people to view their own musical system as "natural" rather than culturally constructed.

In the West, people have attributed consonance—the perception that certain notes sound good together—to such universal forces as mathematics or the physics of the inner ear. Yet the Tsimané, an isolated Amazonian society with little exposure to Western culture, were shown to rate consonance and dissonance as equally pleasant. Despite evidence that culture plays a critical role in shaping aesthetic responses to music, something about the ease and power of musical communication makes it difficult for people to imagine that their own fundamental responses to sound are not universally shared. This divide between perceived naturalness and actual cultural dependency is precisely what allows music such tremendous force: it transmits messages about culture and identity while feeling direct and unmediated.

Certain characteristics are broadly or universally shared among musical cultures throughout the world. Cultures tend to recognize pitches an octave apart as equivalent, and they divide the space between them into scales. Scales tend to apportion the octave unevenly, making it easier to build rich hierarchic musical structures. The most common interval between pitches tends to be small—about the size of the interval formed by two adjacent keys on a piano. At least some of the music in every known culture is metric—based on the regular pattern of a beat—and these beats often group into twos and threes. Music usually takes place in discrete, repeatable acts, such as the performance of a song, and repetition tends to play a major role at multiple levels of musical structure. Two songs can be recognized as the same even when they are transposed—modified to start at a different pitch level— as long as the pattern of the relationships between the notes stays the same.

Music occurs frequently in contexts of ritual and play. Many cultures recognize its capacity to induce particular states of mind, and to create a special atmosphere when groups assemble. Worldwide, people experience music much more frequently in groups than alone. Music is often perceived as expressive in ways that go beyond language. Music can seem deeply meaningful even when it does not denote a concrete object or idea; rather, it seems to traffic in the ambiguous, the multiple interpretable. Cambridge musicologist Ian Cross has suggested that this quality of "floating intentionality"—the sense that music is about something, but resists pinning down what precisely that something might be—allows for large groups of people listening to or making music to experience the pleasure of a shared communicative experience even though the specific details of their understanding might differ profoundly. Indeed, the sense of being transported beyond one's self tends to be a hallmark of musical listening across the world. This powerful kind of experience has variously been referred to as effervescence, a surplus of affect, or (in less fanciful terms) a heightened state of arousal. Rather than be listened to and merely received, music tends to sweep people into its vicissitudes, eliciting sympathetic movement (toe taps or head nods) or a tacit sense of participation (mentally singing along, or feeling drawn out of yourself and into the music).

This capacity underlies what Durham ethnomusicologist Martin Clayton identifies as the four primary functions of music: to regulate a mental or physiological state, to mediate between self and other, to function as symbols, and to help coordinate action. Despite the fact that diverse musical traditions all tend to enact these functions, they marshal very different sonic materials to do so. Only one musical genre tends to use the same features from one culture to another: the lullaby. All over the world, lullabies tend to feature higher pitch levels, a slower pace, and a warmer vocal tone. Lullabies recorded by a parent in the presence of an infant entrance babies more successfully than lullabies recorded in the absence of one—suggesting that certain vocal qualities emerge automatically when parents interact with infants. This is true not only for lullabies, but also for infant-directed speech—the special way adults tend to talk to babies. They slow their speech down, exaggerate its prosody, and use more repetition—all changes that infuse speech with more music-like qualities. Infants respond preferentially to these modifications; they like speech that has been musicalized in this way. The fundamental role that music plays in people's earliest social experiences tends to support a vision of humans as essentially musical.

The musical brain

A logical first place to look for this essential human musicality is the brain. As neuroimaging tools have evolved during the first part of the twenty-first century, it has become possible to identify the regions of the brain that engage when performing particular tasks, such as listening to music. A reasonable initial expectation might have been that neuroimaging would uncover a music center—a distinct anatomical region of the brain devoted to processing music. Instead, what emerged was evidence that music relies on an especially diffuse array of neural circuitry. Rather than depending on a single dedicated region, the ability to hear, understand, and make music calls on networks spread throughout the brain—networks used by many other activities from speech to movement planning. This overlap likely explains some of the benefits musical experience and training can confer on abilities as diverse as learning a second language, literacy, executive function, and social and emotional processing.

One of the best-studied characteristics associated with early music training is a thicker corpus callosum. The corpus callosum is a bundle of nerve fibers that connects the left and right sides of the brain. Speculative interpretations of this finding point to the multiplicity of regions subserving musical experience, and argue that one of the important benefits of learning music is improving communication between different parts of the brain. This makes intuitive sense because playing an instrument involves perceptual skills such as distinguishing different pitches, motor skills such as coordinating arm movements, visual skills such as reading music or watching other members of an ensemble, cognitive skills such as interpreting a piece's structure, emotional skills such as interpreting the expressive aspects of a melody, social skills such as working with a teacher or conductor, and executive skills such as planning a practice session. In other words, what might be special about music is not so much that it is different from everything else, but rather that it draws everything else together.

On the other hand, it is impossible to conclude from existing research whether music training leads to a thicker corpus callosum, or whether people with a thicker corpus callosum are likelier to seek out music training in the first place. The only way to know for sure would be to engage in a longitudinal study, scanning children's brains before the onset of music training and again, as adults, at the end of it, yet studies like this are expensive and logistically complex. Accordingly, much of the research on the effect of music training on the brain is correlational rather than causal in nature—it identifies an association between training and specific characteristics, but it cannot confirm whether training actually caused the effect.

Listening to music often seems effortless and unmediated. Within a fraction of a second, we can recognize a song that was popular during our childhood or sense a specific and difficult-to-articulate kind of sadness within a melody. Yet these impressions begin as physical phenomena—the vibration of eardrums, which displaces the tiny bones behind them, which perturbs the fluid in the inner ear, which, in turn, moves hair cells, sending electrical signals up the auditory nerve. These signals pass through several waystations that refine the signal, combine information from both ears to compute the location of the sound, modulate reflexes such as the startle response, and integrate acoustic information with information from other modalities, such as vision, before reaching the cortex—the folded outer layer of the brain that gives rise to awareness and higher-level thought and perception.

The primary auditory cortex is located along the sides of the brain near the ears, on the superior temporal gyrus in the temporal lobe. This region is larger in people with extensive musical training: not surprising, given the cortex's plasticity, or tendency to change with use and experience. But cells in the brainstem also track properties of sound more accurately in people who have had music training. Because this part of the brain, often referred to casually as "reptilian," is one of the oldest in humans, having evolved millions of years ago to regulate essential functions such as breathing and heartbeats, it is particularly startling to learn that musical experience might be able to enhance aspects of its functioning.

Although the primary auditory cortex is responsible for tasks such as recognizing pitch, many of the behaviors we think about as distinctly musical, such as following a beat or attending to the expressive qualities of a song, rely on circuitry that extends far beyond it. The motor cortex, responsible for the planning and execution of voluntary movements, also engages when people listen to music, even when they are sitting still. This finding supports the notion that music can elicit experiences of imagined movement, pulling listeners into its orbit and involving even stationary listeners in a sense of sympathetic physical engagement. The basal ganglia, clusters of neurons located underneath the cortex, oversee goal-directed action sequences, movement patterns that form parts of ingrained habits, and action learning. They also contribute critically to processing beat-based music—music with the kind of temporal characteristics that allow listeners to clap along and predict the timepoint at which future events will happen. Electronic dance music, for example, encourages this kind of involvement and temporal prediction, but medieval plainchant does not. In plainchant, the notes amble around without the kind of temporal regularity that would allow listeners to orient precisely to when the next note should occur.

Peak emotional responses to music have also received substantial attention from cognitive neuroscience. When music triggers intense pleasure accompanied by a sensation of chills, or shivers down the spine, reward circuitry, including the ventral striatum, orbitofrontal cortex, and ventral medial prefrontal cortex, deploys. Ecstatic experiences of food and sex activate the same circuitry, but, in those cases, it is easier to imagine evolutionary pressure incentivizing the behavior. The release of the neurotransmitter dopamine plays a key role in the reward system. When listening to music, dopamine releases not only during the most intensely pleasurable moment, but also during the moments leading up to it, signaling the critical role of anticipation and prediction even in passive listening.

Neuroscientific studies of music show substantial overlap between music and language processing. Working memory for music and speech seems to rely on the same neural underpinnings, and some argue that the structural, rule-based aspects of music are supported by the same regions that support the processing of grammar in language.

It is difficult not to notice how deeply musical processing integrates with other aspects of human functioning, from movement to motivation. This functional overlap and the brain's fundamental plasticity—or capacity to change—sets up the circumstances by which musical experience can affect a host of other abilities.

Music and health

The notion that music powerfully affects human life and wellness has existed for millennia. In *The Republic*, Plato extolled music training as capable of shaping the soul—and he advocated banning particular scales on the basis that they encouraged drunkenness and laziness. His students are said to have used music to cure nervous disorders ranging from hysteria to seizures. But ideas about music and health circulate not only in the West; cultures the world over integrate music into healing ceremonies. Many people intuitively turn to music to help them feel better or to help them run faster or lift heavier weights. In the United States, a professional organization known as the American Music Therapy Association and, in the United Kingdom, the British Association for Music Therapy, oversee training and research in the therapeutic applications of music.

The overlap of the neural circuitry devoted to music and the neural circuitry devoted to motor control means that the simple act of listening to music can sometimes help people with serious movement disorders. People with Parkinson's disease, for example, experience a kind of slowed movement that makes even simple tasks and getting around difficult. They also suffer from tremors, muscle stiffness, and problems with balance and rigidity. Parkinson's, a degenerative disorder, affects cells in deep parts of the brain, including the basal ganglia. This area also serves as the seat of anticipatory processing for beat-based music. When people with Parkinson's disease listen to rhythmic music, their gait noticeably improves (YouTube features a number of compelling videos capturing gait differences before and during music listening), as does their coordination, posture, and balance. This benefit does not accrue to just any kind of rhythm—it is possible to generate visual rhythms by flashing images, for example, or tactile ones by applying touch pressure in particular temporal patterns—but only in response to auditory rhythms. The auditory system's reaction time is faster by several tens of milliseconds than these other sensory systems, and it is uniquely attuned to temporal regularity and structure. People with Parkinson's disease synchronize their movements to the beat structure in the music, and considerable improvements in gait and coordination can sometimes extend past the end of the therapeutic session.

Neural circuitry devoted to music processing also overlaps with the neural circuitry devoted to speech processing. People who experience damage to the inferior frontal gyrus in the left hemisphere via stroke or traumatic injury can acquire nonfluent aphasia, an extremely frustrating impairment in which language comprehension can be preserved even as the ability to speak fluently is lost. Melodic Intonation Therapy, a well-established treatment for this condition, harnesses the musical aspects of speech to encourage language development within undamaged regions in the right hemisphere. People who cannot produce individual words are taught to sing them and gradually to transition to speaking them without the extra melodic and rhythmic emphasis (a procedure well chronicled on YouTube).

Since therapists ultimately hope to help their patients produce fluent spontaneous speech, they also teach them to generate their own target phrases by tapping their left hand, humming and then softly singing the words, encouraging them to strive to hear the phrase as if it were being sung internally. Many people who graduate from the program attain self-sufficiency and the power to learn additional phrases beyond the study sessions.

Music's colonization of multiple brain areas and pathways helps musical memories survive even when dementia has profoundly disrupted memory systems. Numerous clinical observations suggest that dementia patients can remember and enjoy the music of their adolescence even when they have progressed to advanced stages of the disease. Moreover, people with serious cognitive impairments can continue to identify the emotional resonance of musical selections. Some claim that these episodes of successful musical remembering can improve cognitive functioning on non-music-related tasks in the moments during and immediately after the experiences.

Very basic connections between music and health are reinforced by data showing that babies in neonatal intensive care units (NICUs) with background music eat more food, cry less, sleep better, and require fewer days in the hospital than babies in units without background music. Then again, adults working in the units that play music also report feeling less anxious, which serves as a possible mediating variable—babies' improved outcomes could derive from the capacity of a calmer staff to provide improved care. An alternative hypothesis for music's benefit to NICU babies holds that it provides neurological stimulation essential to development and recovery that struggling babies lack the energy to obtain in other ways.

For people of all ages, relaxing music can produce distinct physiological effects ranging from lowered blood pressure to a slower pulse. When people listen to music they enjoy, their pain tolerance improves, as measured by such behaviors as the length of time they're willing to keep their hand immersed in extremely cold water. Yet these effects are clearly mediated by culture and experience, since music that can be highly pleasurable to one group can be highly obnoxious—even traumatic—to another, or to the same people in a different circumstance. Guantánamo Bay prisoners were subjected to recordings of Metallica as a form of torture, and during the 1990s siege of its Waco, Texas, compound, members of the Branch Davidian sect were subjected to Andy Williams albums for the same purpose.

Are nonhuman animals musical?

At first glance, humans seem to be the only musical animals. Our closest evolutionary relatives, the great apes, do not spontaneously indulge in behaviors we would recognize as musical. Primates do not show a consistent preference for music over silence, or for consonant, pleasant-sounding music over music that is dissonant and perceived by Western listeners as discordant.

Yet a closer examination reveals that different species possess in isolation some of the building blocks that together constitute musicality. For example, gorillas, chimpanzees, and macaques drum by clapping their hands or banging on trees, logs, or their own chests, and woodpeckers drill with their beak. A host of different species, including songbirds, parrots, hummingbirds, seals, elephants, bats, and whales, exhibit vocal learning—the ability to acquire new vocalizations through imitation. This ability relates particularly closely to musicality because it depends on a key link between the auditory system, which is devoted to perceiving and representing sound, and the motor system, which is devoted to reproducing it. This connection between the auditory and the motor systems also critically underlies the human musical capacity. Like humans, all three bird species that exhibit vocal learning possess direct neural pathways between auditory and motor regions that species without vocal learning do not possess.

Several other species exhibit group synchrony—large groups of male fireflies can flash in time with each other; large groups of male frogs, cicadas, and crickets can synchronize, or entrain, their mating calls to generate a noisy chorus. This capacity to orient together in time also underlies the human ability to tap along to a beat or play with an ensemble. The animals that display parts of the musical capacity, ranging from crickets, seals, and songbirds to chimpanzees, clearly do not occupy a single branch of the evolutionary tree. Presumably, these abilities arose independently in different species rather than via inheritance from a shared ancestor. The fact that humans' closest relatives do not display more of the component abilities than more distant relatives implies that no simple and unambiguous path for the evolution of musicality exists.

Some case studies of animal musicality have aroused special interest. In the 2000s, a YouTube clip of a cockatoo named Snowball dancing to a Backstreet Boys song was brought to the attention of Aniruddh Patel and John Iversen at the Neurosciences Institute in La Jolla, California. They set out to systematically study whether Snowball could spontaneously synchronize to a beat without relying on visual cues from a trainer. They played Snowball's favorite song at several different speeds and video recorded his movements, analyzing their peaks and troughs and measuring their degree of alignment with the underlying beat. Snowball was indeed able to synchronize his movements to different musical beats: a remarkable demonstration of an animal's capacity to perform a task previously thought to be relegated to humans. His ability to modulate his movements in response to auditory timing patterns demonstrates the kind of auditory-motor connections thought to be essential to musicality in humans.

Also startling were findings that pigeons could be trained to correctly categorize by pushing the correct button, with their beak, new musical excerpts as originating from Stravinsky's

Rite of Spring or a Bach composition for organ, and that carp could be trained to categorize new musical excerpts as blues or classical. Striking as these results seem, they do not imply that fish and birds possess aesthetic sensibilities. Rather, they demonstrate that some fish and birds can detect the basic acoustic features that distinguish musical genres, such as the presence or absence of an organ or a bass guitar. The pigeons need not have abstracted stylistic features or information about the scale system, for example, to perform the task.

The temptation to overinterpret these studies provides an important reminder about the scientific examination of cultural phenomena—interpretation should proceed carefully from the precise manipulations in the study, remaining mindful of potential confounds. Further experimental work can resolve outstanding questions. For example, rerunning the pigeon and carp studies with MIDI transcriptions of the stimuli, so that the instrumentation did not vary between Stravinsky and Bach or between blues and classical, could determine whether the categorization relied on low-level acoustic cues. Once the surface feature of instrumentation was stripped away, the birds and fish would presumably no longer be able to discriminate between the categories.

One songbird species, the bullfinch, has been known to demonstrate especially prodigious abilities. A particularly enterprising bullfinch was able to learn a forty-five-note tune from its trainer and perform it accurately at the original pitch level. Other bullfinches can sing in alternation with a trainer, waiting their turn to continue a tune after the human sings an intervening part. These achievements represent impressive learning not only in terms of relative pitch (the capacity to abstract the forty-five-note pattern and reproduce it at another pitch level), but also in terms of timing and anticipation (the ability to wait through the human's part of the melody and enter with the appropriate continuation).

The evolutionary origins of music

Evidence from comparative studies of different species does not tell a compelling story about music's evolutionary history. No clear incremental path through different species traces the acquisition of individual components leading to full-blown musicality in humans. Similarly, there is no smoking gun, such as a distinct brain structure or particular set of genes, that unambiguously demonstrates a biological basis for music. It is not surprising, then, that some have rejected the idea that natural selection directly shaped the musical capacity at all, viewing music instead as a human invention exploiting biological apparatuses that evolved for other purposes. Evolutionary psychologist Steven Pinker encapsulated this perspective when he referred to music as "auditory cheesecake." Just as a specific taste for cheesecake did not evolve—rather, cheesecake exploits underlying proclivities for sugar and fat—he argues that aptitude for music did not arise from evolutionary pressure. Instead, he suggests, musicality relies on other capacities that evolved to support more clearly survival-enhancing functions.

People who believe that the ability to make and enjoy music has a more direct biological basis point to several ways that these capacities might have been adaptive. Music facilitates social bonding, potentially resulting in the evolutionary advantage of tighter-knit and more effective groups. Music modulates infant arousal states, potentially resulting in the evolutionary advantage of babies who could flourish while their parents used their hands to perform other useful tasks. Music helps people sync their behavior and attention in time, potentially resulting in the evolutionary advantage of better coordinated labor. Perhaps the capacity for music arose through sexual selection, like the peacock's tail (although the fact that musicality characterizes both genders in all known cultures seems to argue against this notion).

What does seem clear from surveying the diversity of musical practice around the world and the diversity of brain structures required to support it is that music itself encompasses a host of individual components; accordingly, its evolutionary history is likely to encompass a variety of stages and mechanisms. When people think about evolution, they often think about adaptation, the process by which a particular trait that confers a survival advantage gradually becomes dominant within a population. But other processes contribute as well. Sometimes, in a process called exaptation, a trait that evolved because it conferred a particular benefit ultimately enables a new and helpful function for which it was not originally selected, and this new function drives further evolution. In other cases, a particular, selected-for trait brings along a by-product that does not affect evolutionary trajectories; it merely "comes along for free" with the original characteristic. These by-products are called spandrels.

The emergence of the capacity for music likely involved adaptations, exaptations, and spandrels at different stages—a messy supposition that belies the aspirations of people who would seek to justify music's cultural role by attributing it to biology. Music is worthy of interest and support, the argument goes, because evolution wrote it into our genes. But need this simplistic account really be recruited to buttress the merits of a behavior that spans the world and moves so many so profoundly? A bit of devil's advocacy may help illuminate the point: even if music were 100 percent spandrel, having arisen through no direct selective pressure, its reliance on so many biological substrates, its global universality, and its substantial societal power all make the case for sustained inquiry into this distinctively human art.

Chapter 3
Music as language

Music can feel like it communicates powerfully. Is music actually some sort of language? If so, what does it mean and how does it convey these meanings? What would it take to be fluent in music? Do musical grammars work the same way as linguistic grammars?

Indeed, some similarities between music and language seem striking. As communicative systems, they both feature some universal components and much cultural variation. Both consist of complex auditory signals that can be (but do not have to be) visually represented in notation. Both can involve interpersonal coordination: to hold a conversation in the case of language, or to play with a group in the case of music. Both combine discrete sound units into rich structures—sentences and paragraphs in the case of language, phrases and sections in the case of music.

Because cognitive psychology had studied language for many years before turning to music, psycholinguistics provided a rich collection of hypotheses, methods, and questions to help frame the nascent cognitive science of music in its earliest stages. Even now, comparing music to language remains seductive as a foundational approach. In the worst case, this can result in a kind of blindness to the aspects of music that do not fit the linguistic model. But more often, it results in something positive: by delineating the ways in which linguistic models fail to transfer, the comparison provides a new framework for thinking about music. The multi-decade inquiry into the relationship between music and language has borne rich fruit.

Musical grammar and musical expressivity

One of the most distinctive elements of language is syntax, the set of rules that governs sentence structure, making "Laura eats broccoli" an entirely different assertion from "broccoli eats Laura." Language involves a set of atomic units—words—that are arranged in conformance with this set of rules so that some combinations that break the rules are incorrect or nonsensical ("eats broccoli Laura"). Like language, music consists of a set of atomic units—individual notes—that are combined according to certain rules. Most people learn the syntactic rules that govern language implicitly, without any formal instruction, simply through everyday exposure as a baby and toddler. Once they enter school, however, they can study these rules in a more explicit way, in grammar classes, for example. Similarly, most people learn the syntactic rules that govern music implicitly, without any formal instruction, simply through everyday listening, although it is possible to take classes in music theory that aim to convey them explicitly.

People who have not taken music classes might assert that they have not learned the supposed rules that govern the ways notes are put together. But anyone who has noticed when a performer played a wrong note or intuited when a piece was about to come to an end has abstracted important parts of the music's underlying structural rules. Take the case of the wrong note. It might pop out as incorrect because it does not belong to the underlying key, or because it makes an awkward leap that does not fit with the governing melodic line. Although most of the time, a wrong note of this sort arises because of performer error, composers will sometimes write them directly into the score, as in the case of twentieth-century Russian composer Sergei Prokofiev's "wrong note" melodies, which purposely emphasize notes that sound like errors. Music theorist David Huron analyzes the theme from Prokofiev's *Peter and the Wolf* to illustrate that these intentional "wrong notes" can be used artistically, to transmit specific expressive properties—in this case, a characterization of Peter as willful or mischievous. Does this flexibility mean that music's rules are more malleable than those of language?

To answer this question, consider the example of the syntactically incorrect utterance used above: "eats broccoli Laura." It is not difficult to think of scenarios in which this expression could be adopted to serve a real communicative purpose. There could be a class, for example, in which two students were named Laura. On the first day, they introduced themselves, including a fun fact to help people in the class get to know each other. The first Laura said she does not eat broccoli. The second Laura joked that she does, in fact, eat broccoli. From then on, the teacher called the second student "eats broccoli Laura." Like the musical example, where the wrong note carries particular expressive associations, this linguistic use of a syntactical mistake conveys a particular attitude: it suggests irreverence and an attempt by the teacher to entertain.

But what about the other linguistic example, where the simple reversal of the first and last words could transform the relatively innocuous description of a woman eating broccoli into the horror-movie scenario of broccoli eating a woman? Syntax plays a critical role in determining the meaning of individual sentences. Musical meaning works very differently from language, but syntax plays a similarly important part. To understand this role requires thinking about how structure unfolds in time.

When we listen to speech, we constantly predict what words will come next, and allocate cognitive resources to processing them in advance. This predictive processing is speedy and efficient—it preselects the most likely continuations, so that we do not waste time searching through thousands of possible word representations as the conversation ensues. Once a partner says, "How are," some resources have already been allocated to "you." The classic evidence comes from priming studies, in which people are shown to be reliably faster at performing arbitrary tasks such as counting letters or detecting errors in words that are predictable from the preceding context. For example, people are faster at responding to "dog" than "pig" after the context sentence: "The mail carrier was almost bitten by the ___." Moreover, EEG, a tool for measuring electrical activity in the brain, detects neural signatures of surprise in response to unlikely words.

These findings extend to surprising events in music. Even in listeners with no formal musical training, notes and chords that are unlikely within the established musical context elicit these same EEG signatures. Similarly, reaction times to arbitrary questions like what timbre a note or chord is and whether it is in or out of tune are faster when the note or chord is predictable given the preceding context.

But does the predictability of musical sequences actually make them syntactic? University of Maryland psychologist L. Robert Slevc and colleagues addressed this question by playing people chord sequences as they read sentences. Both the musical and the linguistic stimuli featured some kind of predictive violation, but the violation was not always syntactic. For example, a syntactic musical violation might involve a chord drawn from outside the key, but a non-syntactic violation could involve the sudden occurrence of a chord played by flutes after a succession of chords played by violins. Only in the cases where syntactic musical violations happened at the same time as syntactic language violations were reaction times excessively slowed, suggesting that syntactic violations in music and language draw on the same finite neural resources. People disagree about exactly what these resources might be. Instead of supporting syntactic processing in particular, they might undergird more general processes such as error detection or aspects of memory.

Regardless of the precise nature of these cognitive resources, the ability to form expectations about impending musical events makes unique expressive functions possible. As people listen to music, they find some moments tense and unresolved and other moments calm and full of resolution. These impressions fluctuate dynamically as the music progresses. In one well-established method for studying these perceptions, people move a slider continuously in real time, as a piece of music plays, pushing it forward as they perceive the tension to build and pulling it back as they perceive the tension to recede. Surprises—moments where the music does something the listener did not predict—tend to elicit impressions of high tension. Conversely, listeners tend to experience moments where the music takes the expected path as less tense and more relaxed.

This anticipatory engagement has been shown to activate the dopamine system, one of the best understood parts of the brain's reward circuitry. This link between the syntactic structure of music and subjective experiences of its expressivity is tantalizing because it accounts for parts of our difficult-to-articulate musical sensations in terms of objective structural features.

Learning in music and language

How do people acquire expertise with musical syntax in the absence of explicit training? In both music and language, exposure to a particular system suffices to give people implicit knowledge of its structure—knowledge that cleverly designed experiments can expose, but that people may not be able to articulate. Just as a baby born in Beijing will acquire competence in Chinese but a baby born in Paris will acquire competence in French, babies can acquire the syntax of Indian classical music or

Western classical music or both, depending on what they are exposed to.

In the 1960s, the linguist Noam Chomsky proposed that infants could not possibly learn language so rapidly unless they possessed an innate language mechanism that predisposed them to learning particular kinds of grammar and structural relations. In the early 1980s, the composer Fred Lerdahl and the linguist Ray Jackendoff adapted this theory to music, arguing that the kinds of hierarchy that underlie linguistic structure also underlie musical structure. Chomsky's tree structure analyses, in which every word could be assigned a role that clarified its function within the sentence, could be placed side by side with Lerdahl and Jackendoff's tree structure analyses of musical phrases, in which every note could be assigned a role that clarified its function. The two trees looked remarkably similar.

During the 1990s, a set of studies using both speech and music seemed to suggest that a simpler mechanism might contribute to the rapid implicit learning characteristic of both domains. These studies began with a fundamental question: how do infants learn to segment the speech stream into words? Think about the experience of listening to a foreign language. One of the toughest initial barriers to learning is figuring out where one word stops and the next begins.

To simulate this situation, psychologist Jenny Saffran and colleagues played eight-month-old babies continuous strings of syllables—think "ba-la-do-ni-sa"—with no differentiation except for the transition probabilities between the syllables. There were no pauses, for example, or accented syllables of the sort that might indicate boundaries. Unbeknownst to the babies, the researchers had structured the speech stream so that it was composed of three-syllable pseudowords such as "ba-la-do." The only thing that defined pseudowords was the likelihood of one syllable to progress to the next. Within a pseudoword, the probability was 100 percent—"ba" was always followed by "la," which was always followed by "do." But any pseudoword could follow any other one, meaning that after the last syllable of one pseudoword, the transition probability to the next syllable was not 100 percent. In fact, the transition probability between "do," the last syllable of the pseudoword "ba-la-do," and "ni," the first syllable of the next pseudoword, was only 33 percent. Nothing aside from this change in the probability of syllable succession distinguished pseudowords. It seemed like babies were just hearing a very long string of syllables.

Yet in a subsequent test, the infants could distinguish three syllable successions that formed pseudowords from three syllable successions that did not, revealing that they had tracked the statistical characteristics of the audio to which they had been exposed. Clearly, infants did not track these statistics overtly— they could not tell a researcher that "do" followed "la" 100 percent of the time; rather, they absorbed them implicitly, without even trying, a feat adults can perform as well.

Research using undifferentiated strings of notes instead of syllables revealed that musical learning works similarly. Both infants and adults were able to abstract the probability for one note to follow another from simple exposure to a series of tones. This propensity to store statistical information about acoustic events seems to undergird the ability of people to acquire competence in music and language simply through immersion, in the absence of formal instruction.

The kind of competence people ultimately acquire tends to differ between language and music. Most people effortlessly acquire the ability to both understand and produce speech. In the case of music, however, most people acquire the ability to listen and understand, but require more specialized instruction to play an instrument or sing. This difference may stem not from some essential dissimilarity between language and music, but rather from cultural differences in their prevalence and usage. Whereas most babies are invited into active dialogue with conversation partners, a smaller number are invited into regular musical interactions during daily life. Researchers continue to investigate the reasons that music-making ability is distributed more variably in the population than speaking ability, with some attributing it to culture and others to biology.

Musical meaning

At one level, language is comprised of words whose meanings are capable of being listed in a dictionary. No comparable level of music analysis seems to provide an analog to this kind of dictionary lookup. But the allure of linguistic comparison has enticed some scholars to try and find one. In the 1950s, musicologist Deryck Cooke pursued the interval—the distance between two pitches—as the atomic level of musical meaning. He painstakingly paged through scores of vocal music, identifying the words that tended to be set to each interval, and argued that these constituted their conventional meanings. He concluded, for example, that the minor sixth expresses "active anguish in the context of flux."

Common sense suggests, however, that the notion of a linguistic semantics does not translate to music so straightforwardly. I do not, for example, experience a melody as a succession of intervals with specific real-world meanings. Yet clear extra-musical associations do exist. Stefan Koelsch used EEG to demonstrate that target words could be brought to mind by a musical excerpt as easily as by a spoken sentence. For example, a church hymn could make a listener imagine the word "devotion."

Researchers at the University of Arkansas played people wordless orchestral excerpts they had not heard before and asked them to provide free-response accounts of any story they had imagined while listening. This is an alarmingly unconstrained task—researchers expected responses to be wildly divergent and subjective. Instead, for many of the excerpts, a majority of respondents used the same words in their stories, often words drawn from cinematic associations. For example, after an excerpt by Liszt that itself had never been used in a cartoon, the majority of people described a story featuring scurrying mice, two characters chasing one another, a cat and a mouse, or (most specifically) Tom and Jerry. After a relatively obscure excerpt by eighteenth-century composer Telemann, 88 percent of freely constructed narrative descriptions used one of these words that connote a grand affair: ballroom, dance, celebratory event, fancy party, or royal wedding.

Response agreement in this study extended beyond the specific words used to characteristics like verb tense, with some excerpts eliciting descriptions of events that were already happening, and some eliciting descriptions of events that were about to happen in the future. It is striking that music, typically thought of as relatively abstract, triggers immediate concrete associations to listeners within a particular culture. Advertisers can take advantage of these relationships, both by seeking to align their product with a particular tune or style and by trying to evoke associations not overtly stated within the commercial.

Despite new discoveries about music's capacity to refer to nonmusical entities, these semantic associations are not what most people think about when they mention musical meaning. Often, they are thinking instead about how music comes to acquire significance in their lives, and why it matters to them. The same song can mean very different things to someone who met his girlfriend while listening to it and someone who broke up with his girlfriend while listening to it. Leonard Cohen's "Hallelujah" has been used in dozens of television shows and movies, and at public events ranging from the state funeral in Canada of Official Opposition leader Jack Layton to the first episode of *Saturday Night Live* following the 2016 US presidential election. One particular piece of music can take on a wide range of emotional resonances, depending on the context and the prior experiences of the listener.

One of the ways that music can be understood to communicate or mean something comes from its capacity to imaginatively engage the motor system, energizing a runner with a just-fast-enough beat or sympathetically wrapping the listener into the mournful contours of a solo cello line. Instead of approaching a series of sounds as pointers to some extra-musical, real-word meaning, musical listening often involves imaginatively inhabiting the sounds themselves, and orienting first to their sonic qualities rather than to some other concept for which they stand. People sometimes describe this as a kind of communication that goes beyond words, into the grain of experience itself.

But as with language, even this kind of meaning is highly dependent on culture. Neuroscientist Patrick Wong and colleagues found that listeners raised in a rural part of Bihar, India, with little access to Western classical music and listeners raised in Chicago, Illinois, with little access to Indian classical music not only showed decreased recognition memory for excerpts from the other culture, but also responded significantly differently to tasks related to basic expressive engagement—for example, their impressions of tension in music from the unfamiliar culture did not match those of native listeners. Listeners raised in Chicago by Indian parents who had been exposed to both Indian and Western classical music since childhood responded similarly to both styles, not differentiating them in terms of memory performance or perceived tension. Musical meaning of all varieties emerges out of a complex interplay between mind and culture.

Music-language interactions

Some people have special experience with music, such as extensive training on an instrument, and some have special experience with language, such as speaking multiple languages fluently. Given the overlaps between the cognitive systems that process speech and music, experience or aptitude in one domain can affect abilities in the other. Early musical training encourages children to attend carefully to sound. They need to listen closely, match pitch, and reproduce temporal sequences. Children with early musical training demonstrate more accurate frequency-following responses from cells in the brainstem whose job it is to relay information about sound to higher processing centers. Adults who studied music during childhood continue to benefit from these higher-fidelity neural responses, even decades after the training has ceased.

The increased accuracy of pitch tracking in the brainstem likely contributes to some of the benefits musical training has been shown to confer on reading ability. Because reading skills depend fundamentally on phonological awareness—the ability to parse and represent the component sounds of a language—the superior auditory processing developed through musical training might help children learn to read or improve a person's ability to understand speech presented in a noisy environment. Yet much of the research on this topic compares children who happen to have received musical training with children who have not, rather than randomly assigning children to a group that will or will not receive training. If children who enroll in music lessons tend to have higher aptitude for auditory processing to begin with, eventual linguistic benefits might accrue from this underlying aptitude difference, rather than from the training itself.

One of the most important components of musical training involves guiding attention in time—engaging with sound anticipatorily to predict when certain events will occur. For example, a student might need to listen closely to understand when to enter during a duet performance. Practice with allocating attention in time might underpin some of the benefits musical training can provide on achievement in other domains. A study involving dozens of children demonstrated that the capacity to reproduce rhythms in kindergarten predicted reading ability in second grade. Additionally, preschoolers who could most successfully synchronize with a beat also scored highest on a battery of pre-reading tests. Musical training is even associated with superior foreign-language learning in adults. Individuals who have had musical training encode linguistic pitch more accurately when listening to an unfamiliar tone language—a language such as Mandarin Chinese or Thai where pitch conveys semantic meaning rather than mere inflection. These benefits can also apply to clinical populations; musical training improves skills in children with reading impairments such as dyslexia.

Music's impact on language processing stems not only from increased engagement with pitch and timing, but also from increased engagement with auditory patterns more generally. People with musical training show superior implicit learning of both musical and linguistic structures. They also exhibit general improvements in executive functions ranging from auditory attention and working memory to executive control—the capacity to set and pursue goals—that may influence their capacity to acquire new languages.

This relationship between musical and linguistic ability seems to be bidirectional. Tone-language speakers perform better on a variety of music perception tasks, such as pitch memory and melodic discrimination, than people who do not speak a tone language. They also track musical pitch more effectively, as do bilinguals, people who speak two languages fluently.

The border between speech and music

Speech and music typically exhibit different timing profiles. The frequencies within speech sounds change rapidly as consonants and vowels succeed one another. The frequencies within musical performances, on the other hand, tend to change more slowly and exhibit more stability. Individual notes are sustained for discrete durations before giving way to the next one. Additionally, music tends to feature a degree of temporal regularity that speaking does not—it is typically much easier, and more socially acceptable, to clap along to a song than to a speech. Yet the border between music and speech is porous and influenced by culture. Steve Reich's string quartet *Different Trains* incorporates snippets of recorded speech, coaxing out their underlying melodies and passing them back and forth among the instruments. Rap artists virtuosically exploit the rhyme and rhythm latent within everyday speech to spin compelling musical performances.

"Twinkle, Twinkle, Little Star" (sung)

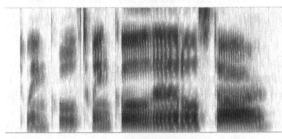

"Twinkle, Twinkle, Little Star" (spoken)

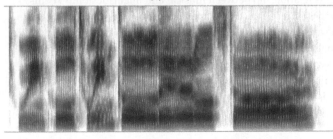

4. Spectrograms are a way of representing sound. The x-axis represents time. The y-axis represents frequency. The darkness of the image represents the amount of energy present at that frequency at that time. The top bar is a spectrogram of a person singing "Twinkle, Twinkle, Little Star." The bottom bar is a spectrogram of the same person speaking the words "Twinkle, Twinkle, Little Star." Frequencies in the sung version are stable for longer periods than in the spoken version.

Several core similarities make it easy to blur these boundaries. Both music and speech tend to be comprised of individual segments (phrases or sentences) that aggregate hierarchically into larger structures (sections or paragraphs). At the end of these segments, sounds tend to descend in pitch and slow down. Particular characteristics, such as speed and pitch height, tend to align with similar expressive functions regardless of whether they occur in speech or music—sounds that are low and slow, for example, tend to be interpreted as sad.

Psychologist Diana Deutsch discovered a striking perceptual illusion that exposes how thin the border between speech and music really is. First, people listen to a full spoken utterance. Then, they hear a short snippet of this utterance (a few words, for example) repeated a number of times. After this period of repeated exposure, they listen to the complete original utterance again. For about 85 percent of people, the snippet that had been repeated now stands out from the rest of the utterance in a dramatic way: it sounds as if it were being sung.

In the speech-to-song illusion, nothing changes about the sequence of sounds. The change occurs in the mind of the listener. After numerous repetitions, the same snippet that had initially sounded like it was being spoken begins to sound like it is being sung. In this scenario, repetition acts as a musicalizing force. And repetition can musicalize more than just speech—looping makes random sequences of tones sound more musical as well, as well as snippets of environmental sound. After a few exposures, the plips and plops of dripping water or the screeches of a shovel being dragged across a rock can come to sound like purposeful musical acts, with foregrounded rhythm and pitch.

Musical structures tend to include much more repetition than linguistic ones. Choruses in pop songs, for example, recur many times without apparent detriment to their position on the charts. If your conversation partner repeated himself with similar frequency, however, it would ordinarily be unpleasant. Repetition encourages a participatory orientation with the sound—a central component of musical attending that may be less critical to language perception. After a number of exposures, a listener knows what is coming next, and can anticipate and even sing along with it. This quality of listening *with* the sound rather than listening *to* it is particularly emblematic of the special kind of engagement we bring to music.

After listening to a speech, verbatim memory of the individual words used is often quite poor. Instead, gist memory—for the actual content conveyed—tends to be elevated. Spoken words sometimes function as mere conduits for the real object of interest: the semantic meaning. Musical experiences usually are not able to be summarized in this way—the nuances and textures of their individual constituent sounds cannot be discarded in favor of some abstract content they are conveying.

Repetition can force listeners to attend to new parts of sounds they have already heard, increasing their engagement with the sonic materials themselves and accordingly with the musical aspects of the presentation. Ordinary speech can take advantage of this musical potential with alliteration, repetition, and special melodic and rhythmic emphasis. This happens with special frequency in public oration and call and response preaching. Martin Luther King Jr.'s "I Have a Dream" speech uses its repeated chorus and dynamic swells to urge the audience into shared resolve. Speech like this can be thought of as adopting musical strategies to encourage a sense of participation and shared intent.

Chapter 4
Listening in time

Music unfolds dynamically, note by note, moment by moment. A performance cannot be taken in all at once; listeners must orient to each passing musical moment using memory systems to reconstruct events that have passed, perceptual systems to take in events that are presently sounding, and predictive mechanisms to anticipate what might happen next. All of these systems affect the experience of *when* each individual event occurs, and the capacity of successive *whens* to cohere into particular temporal perceptions, such as a beat, a rhythm, a beginning, or an ending.

Perceiving meter and rhythm

One of the most distinctive temporal experiences in music is meter—the sense that certain time points within the ongoing musical flow acquire special status as beats. Time points that function as beats succeed one another at roughly equal temporal intervals. Some of the beats feel strong and some feel weak, often following one another in a strong-weak (duple) or strong-weak-weak (triple) pattern.

Auditory cues influence which time points act as beats. For example, a moment that is particularly loud and features an especially low note is likelier to function as a beat, especially if other moments preceding it at regular temporal intervals were similarly accented. But acoustic features alone cannot explain the perception of meter. Many kinds of evidence point to the active role of the human mind in generating metric experience.

For one thing, even sounds that possess no acoustic differentiation at all—ticks that inform the driver when she has activated the turn signal, for example—can undergo perceptual transformation and seem to alternate between strong and weak beats, occasionally triggering head bobs that imply the driver is enjoying dance music rather than just trying to make a turn. This phenomenon, termed subjective rhythmization, illustrates the way the mind can generate meter even in the absence of compelling acoustic cues.

For another, some passages are metrically ambiguous—they can be heard as either duple or triple, for example. People can be primed to hear the accents as occurring every two beats or every three by listening to an earlier passage featuring duple or triple meter, or merely by imagining a duple or triple meter in advance. Simply by adjusting their mindset, in other words, people can actually hear different accent patterns.

Once people start perceiving a particular meter, acoustic cues have a tough time derailing them. When a meter has been strongly established, for example, the insertion of a pause in the right spot will result in the perception that the silence itself is accented rather than that the meter has changed. Even inserting jaunty off-beat accents does not cause the perceived meter to shift into alignment with these new emphases; instead, people stubbornly cling to the original pattern, allowing the new accents to crackle as syncopations. Ubiquitous in contemporary pop music, syncopations are moments of emphasis that proceed out of phase with the underlying beat; this mismatch gives them a particular quality of punchiness and danceability.

Of all music's features, in fact, meter seems to be most closely linked with bodily movement. Neuroimaging shows that aspects of the motor system are activated by music with a beat—but not by music without one. People agree widely on which musical excerpts arouse a pleasurable drive to move. These excerpts, termed "high-groove," elicit spontaneous rhythmic movements as well as more accurate couplings between body movements and the music's temporal structure.

Meter relies on hierarchical organization. To get a sense of this hierarchy, imagine a group of people clapping along to a song. These claps articulate a privileged metric level, the one to which people synchronize most easily. But with concentration, it might also be possible to tap your foot every two claps or nod your head every four. These foot taps and head nods represent higher levels of the metric hierarchy. Beats at the level to which people clap most readily tend to occur every 600 milliseconds. This works out to around 100 beats per minute (bpm), the unit by which music's tempo, or speed, is often measured. Many pieces have a tempo that falls somewhere between 60 and 120 bpm. This preferred range matches the rate at which people typically walk, hearts usually beat, and breastfeeding newborns normally suckle.

People interact with these levels of temporal organization predictively, actively anticipating events at future timepoints. When people are asked to tap along with metronome clicks, they perform quite accurately (even more so in response to richer musical contexts), but they do not synchronize precisely at the clicks—instead, they tap 20 to 60 milliseconds before them. Listeners engage in anticipatory processing, targeting their attention ahead to the points in time at which they expect musical events to occur. They register tempo changes and judge duration more accurately when presented with several temporal intervals in succession rather than one in isolation, because the series enables them to make predictions. The clearer the temporal patterning the music establishes, the easier it is to project that patterning forward and form specific expectations.

The strongest evidence for metric perception as a way of directing attention to particular points in time is the discovery that people detect pitch changes more easily when they occur on strong beats. Presumably, this perceptual benefit accrues because people direct attention to anticipated beats before they occur. It is possible to flip this logic around and argue that this anticipation actually defines metric accent: beats are timepoints toward which people allocate special anticipatory focus. This perspective has practical ramifications for performers—it suggests that they might be able to fudge a bit of the passagework in a complicated section so long as they get the notes on the strong beats correct. It also has more philosophical ramifications, illuminating the means through which music might synchronize temporal orientation in large groups of people, contributing to their sense of bonding and communion at public concerts.

Perceptual limits constrain how we hear music in time. When less than 100 milliseconds separate musical events (when they follow one another at a rate faster than 10 notes per second), they tend to be experienced as a single continuous sound rather than a series of individual ones, or as a series of events of uncertain length and number. But when more than 1,500 milliseconds separate events, it becomes difficult to maintain a sense of their rhythmic relationship—they seem more like isolated occurrences lacking a palpable rhythmic connection. Many musical events, accordingly, take place in the sweet spot between 100 and 1,500 milliseconds.

Composers can purposefully toy with these limitations, however. Twentieth-century artist Conlon Nancarrow wrote a piece for player piano called Canon X in which one voice starts at the reasonable rate of 4 notes per second and the other starts at the somewhat less reasonable rate of 39 notes per second. Gradually across the course of the piece, the fast voice slows down and the slower voice speeds up, ultimately reaching a speed of 120 notes per second—a speed physically impossible for human fingers to execute but no problem at all for the mechanics of a player piano.

People usually have a clear sense of whether the music they are listening to is fast or slow. This effortless perception originates not only from the number of beats occurring per minute, but also from the number of events occurring per beat. Experiences of physical movement in the world also influence tempo judgments. Children prefer faster tempos than adults. Tempo preference slows gradually across adulthood and into old age.

Aside from the perception of meter and tempo, the most salient aspect of musical time is rhythm. Notoriously difficult to define, rhythm involves perceptions about how the durations of musical events—short or long—relate to one another and to the metric framework within which they unfold. The timing of event onsets influences rhythm more than the timing of other attributes (how long the events are sustained, for example). For events within the 100 to 1,500 millisecond window, succession—what came before what, and what came after—is critically important to perception, as is the duration between event onsets. To get a sense of the importance of these features, imagine a familiar tune like "Happy Birthday." Scrambling the temporal order of the notes would make the tune unrecognizable. So would standardizing the duration between note onsets—ironing out the rhythm so that the note for "you" lasted no longer than the notes for "hap-py."

But it is not just the order of events or the temporal interval between event onsets that determines the rhythmic feel of a piece. It is equally important how these durations hang on the underlying meter. For example, longer notes typically align with strong beats and shorter notes with weak ones—reversing this pattern generates a distinctive energy. Individual musical events cohere into larger groups of events: segments and phrases and sections and pieces. These groups do not necessarily neatly overlay the metric grid. They might start on a strong beat, or before it, leaning in. They might end with a bang on a metric accent or fade out gently on a weak beat. Events' and groups' position with respect to the underlying meter enlivens and animates rhythm.

The temporal emergence of melody and voices

Although psychologists have borrowed many of their models for understanding music from the study of language, they rely on work from visual perception to understand how groups emerge out of sequences of musical events. According to early-twentieth-century Gestalt psychology, people tend to group objects together when they are close to one another, when they are similar, or when they seem to follow the same path. For example, a row of dots separated by a large gap tends to be perceived as two groups, and a row of dots where the first half are white and the second half are black also tends to be perceived as two groups. A visual field full of moving dots where half are moving up and half are moving down tends to be perceived as two composite units, one directed upward and the other downward.

These principles can help explain the perceptual formation of larger entities such as melodies out of individual notes that occur in temporal succession. A series of notes separated by a silent gap will tend to divide into two distinct segments, pre- and post-pause. A series of notes that moves upward by small steps is easier to hear as a unified entity than one that jumps all over the place. Psychologist Albert Bregman applied these insights to help explain the problem of auditory scene analysis: how people parse their soundscape into its constituent parts, picking out the sound of water dripping or a floorboard creaking in a room, or a violin melody or percussive rhythm within a symphony. Examining the mechanisms of psychoacoustics helps clarify why this problem needed solving in the first place.

Sound is transmitted from an originating source—a parent's voice or a recorded flute, for example—to human ears via vibrating columns of air. These vibrations represent the combined activity from all the sound sources within a space. There is not a separate stream of air carrying the voice and another carrying the flute and another the hum of the air conditioner; their contributions all mix together in the composite movement of air columns that ultimately reaches the eardrums. These membranes vibrate, transmitting energy to the tiny bones in the middle ear, which, in turn, generate waves in the fluid inside the cochlea—a curled-up structure along which the basilar membrane is stretched. Different portions of this membrane vibrate selectively in response to specific frequencies. This movement perturbs hair cells, generating electrical activity in the auditory nerve and beginning the signaling chain that ultimately leads to activity in higher processing centers in the cortex and perceptions of sound.

The signal that enters the ear, then, consists of a single wave, representing the sum of all the frequencies generated by the voice and the flute and the air conditioner, but the ultimate auditory perception contains three distinct sound streams. Auditory scene analysis tackles the question of how the ear differentiates individual sound streams with seeming effortlessness from a physical signal that lacks this separation. Just as Gestalt psychologists used images of dots to illustrate the influence of perceptual principles on grouping, Bregman used recordings of sounds to demonstrate how similar principles influence their categorization into distinct streams.

For example, Bregman showed that an alternation between a high pitch and a low pitch can sound like one voice jumping back and forth if played at a moderate speed, but morphs into two distinct voices—one composed of high notes and the other of low ones—if played very fast. Furthermore, the rhythmic impression generated by a pattern of note durations when they are all heard to belong to a single voice disappears when they separate into two streams. When the voices separate, people lose their sensitivity to the rhythmic relationships generated by the succession of high and low notes and orient instead to the rhythmic relationships within each individual voice. Changing the timbre of individual notes—so that some sound reedier, like a wind instrument, for example, and others brassier—can also trigger perceived separation into two streams, one for each timbre.

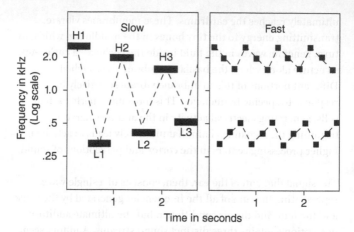

5. When played slowly, a series of high and low pitches sounds like one leaping voice, but when played quickly, it separates into two streams, one made up of high notes and one made up of low notes.

Through numerous demonstrations of this sort, Bregman revealed that people use Gestalt principles such as proximity (in pitch or in time) and similarity (of timbre, for example) to analyze the auditory scene into individual streams. He theorized that these heuristics—basic rules that work enough of the time to be advantageous—for auditory scene analysis arose out of evolutionary pressure; ancestors of modern-day humans would have had to quickly parse a soundscape to determine whether a loud noise came from a predator.

Long before scientists studied the processes that make these perceptual feats possible, composers exploited them to create music. Early-eighteenth-century composers such as Bach, Handel, and Vivaldi pursued Baroque aesthetic ideals by striving for dazzling virtuosity in their work. In works for solo instruments like the violin that can ordinarily play only one melody at a time, the potential for ornate filigree might seem limited. But these composers brilliantly manipulated properties of auditory scene analysis to make it seem as though multiple voices were swirling out of a single instrument. For example, they would insert isolated high notes into a fast passage that otherwise occupied a middle register. Rather than adhere to the rest of the notes, the high ones tended to group together and be heard as a second voice sounding in counterpoint to the first. The beginning of the Allemande from Bach's Violin Partita in B Minor, BWV 1002 serves as a good demonstration of this technique.

East African xylophone music accomplishes a similarly impressive effect by manipulating the order of high and low pitches in duet performances. Because of how these notes move back and forth between cohering and decoupling into separate streams, two performers playing individually simple rhythms can generate an impression of intricate rhythmic complexity.

Like meter, musical grouping occurs at many hierarchic levels. A few notes might group into a distinct segment; a few measures into a phrase; a few phrases into a section; and so forth. People's capacity to perceptually apprehend these groups varies according to the memory system they depend on. Because auditory sensory memory does not extend past about five seconds, it is difficult to directly experience rhythmic relationships that extend beyond this timescale. Larger-scale temporal relationships—such as form— tend to be perceived in a less sensory, more cognitive way.

To illustrate this distinction, think about the difference between the way you hear the rhythm in the hook of your favorite song— that catchy bit that recurs in multiple places—and the way you hear the rhythm of the chorus's reappearances. The hook, no more than five seconds long, is made up of a succession of short and long events whose rhythmic relationships seem as though they are felt more than thought about. The form of the song, on the other hand, spanning more like three minutes, might be composed of verses alternating with choruses. Although it is possible to think back over a song and have a sense of the temporal relationship between occurrences of the chorus and the material surrounding it, the durational relationships of sections are less sensorially available and more reliant on explicit memory, cognition, and auditory imagination (thinking back on and trying to rehear something you heard earlier).

The extent to which musical events that occur at the beginning of a piece influence the way listeners experience musical events near the end is a matter of some controversy. On the one hand, after listening twice to pieces of classical music, people with and without musical training were able to roughly identify whether individual segments had come from the beginning, the middle, or the end. On the other hand, after listening to a Beethoven sonata, university music students were unable to recall whether the exposition (the first major section) of the piece had been repeated or not. They simply did not know whether they had heard that entire section once or twice. Moreover, when the sonata was paused before the final two concluding chords, students predicted that it would continue another minute or two. In the absence of the signature two-chord ending formula, nothing about temporal proportion or form signified the piece had arrived at its final moments. Music students learn lots of explicit knowledge about sonata form—the specific sequence of events that typically happen in this sort of piece—that might have clued them in to the fact that the movement's end was imminent, but they seemed unable to integrate this conceptual knowledge with their sensory experience of listening to the music.

Findings like these led philosopher Jerrold Levinson to argue that music depends on present-focused attention—the sense of how the notes that just happened are leading into the notes about to happen—rather than any explicit awareness of larger-scale form. Although this position probably overstates the importance of the small over the large timescale, it offers a useful corrective to music-theoretic traditions that emphasize high-level structure, sometimes to the exclusion of the momentary dynamism that grips and compels so many listeners. From a psychological perspective, it suggests that thinking about the way conceptual knowledge relates to the real-time act of listening, as the music progresses, is an important topic for further study.

If ideas about the perception of musical time get murky at the highest levels, they do the same at the lowest levels. Although anyone who has learned about Western-style rhythmic notation knows that a half note lasts twice as long as a quarter note, no one aside from a computer actually plays them that way. Human performers use expressive timing, shortening or lengthening notes by tens of milliseconds for expressive effect. Even when asked to play straight, with no expressive inflection at all, performers do not achieve the exact whole-number ratios implied by music notation. Listeners are able to detect expressive alterations on the order of 20 to 50 milliseconds, and microtiming nuances of this magnitude can make the difference between a performance that brings its audience to tears and one that leaves them unmoved.

The actual relationships between two durations are continuous—one can be slightly longer than the next, or slightly *slightly* longer, and so forth. Past the 20- to 50-millisecond floor, listeners can hear these relationships as expressive nuance. But when it comes to hearing rhythmic relationships, categorical perception intervenes to snap relationships into familiar small-integer ratio bins: 1 to 2, or 1 to 3, for example. All the myriad possible durational relationships between two notes tend to be perceived as more accurate or less accurate renditions of these small integer ratios. When an initial note lasts 2.2 times as long as a subsequent one, that feels like an expressively stretched 2:1 ratio rather than a precise 2.2:1 ratio. When listeners are asked to clap the durations they have just heard, they tend to correct them back toward these perceived small integer categories.

Early exposure to the acoustic environment—the music we listen to as children—likely gives rise to these defined categories. To invoke a linguistic parallel, the continuum between the "r" sound and the "l" sound divides into two separate categories for babies exposed to English, but merges into a single category for babies exposed to Japanese, in which separate "r" and "l" phonemes do not exist. Similarly, the fact that so much Western music uses small-integer duration rations (with one note twice or three times as long as another, for example) likely drives our tendency to hear complex rhythms as varied instances of these simple categories.

Rhythmic patterns themselves contain the traces of the broader sonic culture out of which they emerge. Some languages, like English, are stress-timed, resulting in a highly variable succession of durations of individual syllables. Other languages, such as French, are syllable-timed, resulting in a more uniform succession of syllable durations. Musical themes from England and France, it turns out, bear the marks of the linguistic environment in which they were composed: English themes contain more durational variability between successive notes, but durations in French themes are more uniform.

Action and perception in music listening

The way human movements synchronize with music has been studied not only using tapping studies, but also using motion capture technology that can track more complex patterns of music-invoked movement, including dance. These studies reveal that different levels in the metric hierarchy are often reflected by simultaneous movement patterns in different parts of the body, with deeper levels involving more time between beats articulated by torso movements, and more surface levels involving less time between beats articulated by limb movements. Yet these metric levels are not equally noticeable; EEG studies suggest that listeners register rhythm and a basic sense of the beat even when they are not paying attention to the music, but that appreciating deeper levels of the metric hierarchy requires sustained attention. Movements that articulate these deeper levels likely draw attention to the parts of the music that define them. Indeed, studies with the very youngest among us show that movement patterns can influence auditory perception.

Jessica Phillips-Silver and Laurel Trainor played seven-month-old infants an ambiguous rhythm that could be heard in duple meter (with accents every two beats) or in triple meter (with accents every three beats). They repeated this rhythm for two minutes while either bouncing the baby every two beats or every three beats. All the babies heard the same auditory rhythm, but they experienced kinesthetic accents implying a duple or triple meter through movement instead of through sound. Later, the babies showed a preference for a new version of the rhythm with auditory accents that matched the pattern previously established by the movements—the babies who had been bounced every two beats preferred the version with auditory accents every two beats, and the babies who had been bounced every three beats preferred the one with accents every three beats. With apparent ease, they had translated information about timing patterns in movement into information about timing patterns in music. Subsequent work showed that adults who bent their knees while listening to the ambiguous rhythm later identified a new version as more similar to the rhythm they had previously heard when the new auditory accents matched the timing established by the movement. Tight links between the motor and auditory systems start early in development and persist throughout the lifespan.

Rhythm activates a host of brain regions traditionally characterized as motor regions: the supplementary motor area, premotor cortex, cerebellum, and the basal ganglia. Studies of how these regions communicate with each other during music listening demonstrate that meter—the presence of a beat— enhances connectivity between auditory and motor areas. Simply seeing a beat, however—for example, a flashing light—does not elicit such swift, accurate mappings to the motor system. Indeed, people tap less accurately to rhythms presented in the visual domain compared to rhythms presented in sound.

Much musical experience throughout the world is active and participatory, but even in traditions like Western classical music where conventions mandate quiet listening, hearing music can elicit profound experiences of imagined movement. This synchronized sensorimotor attending plays a crucial role in music's social importance, hijacking some of the powerful consequences of moving in time with other people. The degree of synchrony in movements between people on a date, for instance, can predict how positively they will rate the evening afterward. Adults who engage in synchronized behavior such as singing, tapping, or walking rather than an unsynchronized behavior are more likely to cooperate with each other afterward, and to rate their companions as more likable. In laboratory settings, people cooperate better with partners and report liking them more if they sing or tap in synchrony rather than out of phase with each other. Toddlers as young as fourteen months are likelier to altruistically assist an experimenter after they have been bounced in synchrony with her, compared to if they have been bounced out of synchrony.

Musical meter provides a scaffold for synchronizing orientation in time not just with a single partner, but also with large groups of people. Music's capacity to foster a sense of deep synchronization with strangers can serve as an important source of its pleasure. The social bonding that arises out of synchronized temporal orientation has also been cited as one of the elements that makes music useful as a therapeutic tool, and even as one of the benefits that drove the evolution of the human capacity for music. Many religions harness the power of music to create these powerful states, some extending the experience to trancing and other varieties of extended consciousness. Musical timing, in myriad overt and subtle ways, arises out of social experiences and, in turn, constructs new kinds of social understanding.

Chapter 5
The psychology of music performance

Performers occupy a special role within contemporary Western musical culture. Pop fans shout the name of their favorite singer, not their favorite songwriter. Professional orchestras, which tend to program the same core repertoire year after year, market their offerings by highlighting star guest performers. One guitarist can play the same notes as another who left the audience bored, but instead bring them to their feet. The psychology of music performance tries to understand this expressive power. Since two individuals can produce markedly different responses by playing the same notes, it is clear that notation fails to capture some of the most critical dimensions of musical communication. What are these dimensions? What does it take to acquire the kind of expertise in manipulating them that top-notch performers possess? How do listeners perceive and respond to them?

Expressivity in performance

The dimensions available for performers to manipulate include timing—stretching some notes and compressing others, resisting the precise integer ratios between durations implied by notation; dynamics—making some notes louder and others softer in more subtle, continuous increments than dynamic markings like *forte* (loud) or *piano* (soft) imply; articulation—altering the attack and the decay of individual notes, starting some all at once, but easing into others, and terminating some suddenly, but letting others fade out; tempo—performing a piece or a section faster or slower; intonation—subtly raising or lowering the pitch while remaining within the general category of the notated pitch (e.g., playing a slightly sharper or flatter C), or gliding into or away from a note; and timbre—playing more brightly or darkly or otherwise changing the sound quality of a note or passage.

Some of these alterations seem to occur in a systematic, almost rule-based fashion at particular moments in the musical structure. For example, it is common for performers around the world to slow down at phrase boundaries, in proportion to the hierarchical significance of the boundary (less if it ends a section and more if it ends an entire piece). This practice mirrors a parallel tendency in conversation. People tend to slow down at the end of utterances, in proportion to the hierarchical significance of the boundary (less if it ends an individual thought and more if it ends a prolonged exchange on a particular topic). These performance tendencies have perceptual ramifications: the same pattern of deceleration, inserted at different moments within a musical phrase, might be quite noticeable in most places, but undetectable at a phrase boundary. The fact that performers slow down there so regularly renders the pattern almost imperceptible.

Similar sorts of rule-based changes occur in response to metric structure. Performers tend to play notes a little bit louder and sustain them a little bit longer when they fall on strong beats. Rule-based changes also occur in response to the tonal structure of the music—the way that individual pitches are organized in response to a governing central pitch, or tonic. Performers tend to raise a pitch—play it slightly sharp—when it functions as an unstable note about to resolve to a higher pitch, but they tend to lower it—play it slightly flat—when it functions as an unstable note about to resolve to a lower one. Other expressive inflections mark grouping boundaries. Performers often alter the dynamics or timbre at the start of a new section, further delineating the boundary. They tend to delay the onset of the first note in the new section too, in effect lengthening the gap between the end of the previous group and the start of the new one.

These rules can be implemented in computer systems to help mechanical performances of music sound less repellently inhuman. But although machines have been able to dispatch the greatest chess players in the world, mastering human expression on the cello, for instance, has proven more elusive. Despite mid-twentieth-century investments in computer music technology intended to preempt the imminent obsolescence of human performers, there is still no Deep Blue equivalent of Yo-Yo Ma.

In some ways, this reflects the amount of expressive variation that is not straightforwardly attributable to rule-based responses to musical structure. After all, if it were possible to feed in a musical structure and churn out the ideal performance, there would be no need for the lively and diverse community of professional cellists the world over. We could just give Yo-Yo Ma, or his computer stand-in, a piece of music and record the performance. But people crave a variety of different performances of the same repertoire— enjoying a Bach Cello Suite played by Ma one day but performed by Alisa Weilerstein or Pablo Casals on another.

Psychologist Bruno Repp sought to measure the expressive inflections made by different performers. He compared performances of the same piano piece by twenty-four professional pianists with international reputations, and ten student pianists who had not yet broken into the international performance circuit. The students' alterations in timing and dynamics were much more similar to each other's than were the alterations made by the professionals. When timing and dynamic variation across all the performances were averaged to generate a hypothetical typical performance, the expressive modifications by the most acclaimed superstars of the piano were, in fact, often the ones most pronouncedly different from this average. One possible engine driving conformity in student performances and variability in professional performances is economic. Students try to prove they can execute conventional interpretations skillfully enough to be accepted as a professional, and professionals try to individuate themselves from phalanxes of other professionals playing the same repertoire. A less cynical explanation holds that renowned artists are renowned precisely because they tap into non-obvious levels of musical structure and non-obvious channels of musical communication.

Follow-up work examining listener preferences for performances suggested that only a small part—as small as 10 percent—of the variance in these preferences could be attributed to differences in expressive timing and dynamics. This is a critical insight, because it suggests that the dimensions being measured in research on the psychology of music performance might not be the right ones. A simple thought experiment reinforces this supposition. Imagine a single note sung by an acclaimed mezzo-soprano or played on a Stradivarius by a renowned violinist. This single note, insufficient to give rise to the patterns of timing and dynamics typically thought to underlie aesthetic response, can seem grippingly expressive.

Other, more difficult-to-measure parts of the acoustic signal, like timbre—the distinct sound quality an individual performer can draw out of an instrument—likely play a bigger role than current research suggests. To get a better sense of what aspects of sound the term "timbre" refers to, think of how different it would sound if Tom Waits and Brian Wilson sang the same pitch; Waits's voice sounds gravelly and guttural, but Wilson's sounds round and pure. Performers can use different techniques to draw out a timbre that is more Waits- or Wilson-like from their instrument. The powerful effects of timbral manipulation represent one of the many ways that actual musical practice poses questions about human communication that science cannot yet address.

The expressive tools performers use often depend on expert manipulation of very subtle, nuanced aspects of sound—pushing an onset tens of milliseconds forward or back, or playing one note slightly louder than another. The capacity to control sound with this precision strains believability. Yet numerous studies have shown that these inflections are intentional. Performances of the same piece by the same instrumentalist show remarkably consistent patterns of expressive variation, even when they are separated by months or years.

Just as composers seek to choreograph expectations, leading listeners to expect particular continuations and then deviating to something different and expressively charged, performers try to marshal their powers to enhance this manipulation of expectations. For example, a performer might delay the onset of an unexpected note, or subtly alter its timbre. The convincing execution of such expressive alterations depends on the performer's intuition about musical structure, and on his or her experience within the relevant musical style. People who have spent years immersed in a particular body of music generate different expectations than people new to the style. Accordingly, performers who expressively emphasize one kind of expectation

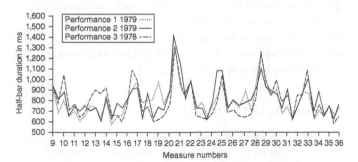

6. These lines show fluctuations in tempo across three different performances by the same pianist of an excerpt from a Chopin étude. The fact that they track each other so closely suggests that expressive variation in microtiming is intentional.

over another might grip a particular kind of listener more persuasively. In this way, understanding expressive performance is more about understanding the dynamic interplay between listener experiences and performer decisions than about understanding how performers relate to a score (the notated version of a piece).

Although much research has examined expressive performance from the perspective of psychology, the bulk of it relates to Western classical music. The degree to which these communicative strategies are shared across different cultures is largely unknown. When musical traditions are oral rather than notated, it can be more difficult to conceptualize and examine performer nuance because the convenient comparative case of an uninflected score does not exist. Sometimes performance choices that count as expressive inflections in one style (for example, altering intonation so that a C is played slightly sharp or flat) can function as entirely different categories in another (for example, in some traditional Indian music, where the pitch range that counts as a C in the West is divided into several distinct individual categories). Similarly, timing categories can vary from culture to culture. To listeners familiar with the even meters of traditional Western music, a performed durational ratio consisting of a slightly longer note followed by a slightly shorter note might be understood as two two-beat notes with the first expressively sustained. To listeners familiar with the uneven meters of traditional Balkan music, however, it might be understood as a three-beat note followed by a two-beat note.

Experiencing performance

In one model for studying listener responses to performer inflection, performers are instructed to play a melody multiple times, aiming to convey a different emotion each time. People then listen to these recordings and attempt to match the performance with the intended emotion. Experiments like this generally show that performer manipulations of dimensions such as timing, dynamics, and articulation can reliably convey basic emotions such as happiness, sadness, or anger. The expressive tools used to convey emotions in music parallel the habits of emotive speech: passages played angrily, just like utterances spoken angrily, tend to be faster and louder and use sharper, more abrupt onsets. Yet studies of this sort are limited by their reliance on basic emotion categories; people often value music for its capacity to transmit complex, nuanced, difficult-to-articulate expressive states.

Researchers also assess listener responses to expressive performance using electrophysiological measures, examining the effect of performer inflections on phenomena like heart rate and skin conductance response (indications of arousal). Most frequently, however, researchers simply ask listeners directly about their experience of a performance. For example, when presented with expressive performances that were closer to or further from average in terms of timing and dynamics, listeners rated the average performances as higher quality, but they rated the less-average performances as more individual. Other studies have revealed a similar disassociation between the kinds of performances listeners find enjoyable and the kinds they find interesting. The link between a performance's averageness and its perceived quality is consistent with research about aesthetic preferences in other domains; for instance, when multiple faces were averaged to form composites, people rated the resultant faces as more beautiful when more faces had been averaged to produce them (when the faces were closer to the true average of a large population). Performer inflections have also been shown to influence listeners' understanding of musical structure, persuading them to hear different meters, phrase boundaries, and climaxes.

But manipulations of the auditory signal are not the only way the performer communicates to the listener. Numerous studies show that information in the visual modality—particularly the movements of performers as they play—has a powerful effect not just on the overall evaluation of the performance, but also on what listeners actually *hear*. This tight coupling between the auditory and the visual domains also characterizes speech. The McGurk effect refers to a perceptual illusion where an audio recording of someone saying "ba-ba-ba" is superimposed on a video recording of the lip movements for "ga-ga-ga." People looking at the video tend to hear an in-between syllable such as "da-da-da," which corrects to "ba-ba-ba" as soon as they close their eyes. Even people who know it is an illusion tend to hear "da-da-da," indicating that visual and audio information integrate automatically, outside of conscious control. What a person sees can fundamentally shape what a person hears.

Numerous examples demonstrate the importance of the visual modality in musical experience. One study suggests that people are able to accurately predict music competition winners by viewing silent videos of their performances, but not by hearing audio recordings of them. The same musical note can be heard as having a more or a less abrupt onset depending on whether it is accompanied by video of a string being plucked (a gesture that typically produces an abrupt onset) or bowed (a gesture that typically produces a more gradual one). The same interval (the distance between two pitches) can be heard as smaller or larger depending on whether it is accompanied by video of a person singing a small or large interval. In fact, people are quite good at judging the size of an interval from video images of people singing them, even when the audio is muted so that they are not hearing anything at all.

People who have watched music videos on MTV or witnessed powerful live performances from close proximity know that these cross-modal effects extend well beyond judgments of onset timing and interval size and into the expressive character of the music. Psychologists William Thompson and Frank Russo showed that people rated dissonant moments (when notes seemed to clash or fail to harmonize with each other) in blues performances by B. B.

King as more dissonant when accompanied by video footage of him visually highlighting the conflict (by narrowing his eyes and shaking his torso, for example) then when they were accompanied by video of him playing with a more neutral facial expression. Perceptions of dissonance contribute essentially to affective responses to music. Scholars have tried to explain them in terms of the structure of the human ear and basic psychoacoustic principles, but research suggests that even something like the raising or lowering of an eyebrow can play a role.

When people are asked to rate the expressive characteristics of musical intervals, the major third (the interval that starts the song "Kumbaya") is often rated as one of the happiest, and the minor third (the interval that starts "Greensleeves") as one of the saddest—despite that they differ by only one semitone. But when audio and video of people singing these intervals are swapped, people experience the sound as conveying different degrees of emotionality. Singers tend to raise their eyebrows, widen their eyes, and spread their mouth into a faint smile when singing a major third. When people see the visual imagery of someone singing a major third while hearing the audio signal from someone singing a minor third, they rate the sound itself as happier.

Musicologist Jane Davidson used motion tracking to capture the movements of violinists while they played either expressively or in a deadpan manner—attempting to convey as little expressivity as possible. Listeners judging the expressive intent of the performer (whether they meant to play with or without expression) were sometimes more accurate when looking at point light displays of the movements than when actually listening to the sound, suggesting that musical expressivity can sometimes be more easily decoded from the visual than the auditory domain. Other work involving clarinetists showed that superimposing video of highly expressive performances on audio from deadpan renditions could convince listeners that the sound itself was full of communicative emotionality. The rich, multidimensional contexts of live concerts likely provide listeners with additional paths to engaging experiences compared to listening over iPods.

Visual information is not the only non-auditory aspect of experience that can influence performance evaluation. Whether or not people read a description of a musical excerpt beforehand can influence how much they enjoy the music. Additionally, when presented with a pair of performances of the same piece, they tend to prefer the second. When people have heard a piece before, they can to process it more efficiently. They tend to misattribute this increased cognitive fluency to some positive characteristic of the music itself, resulting in higher enjoyment ratings for performances that come second. Even when both performances in the pair are acoustically identical, if told they are played by different performers, people will often claim that they sound markedly different, and argue in favor of the second one's superiority.

People also tend to enjoy individual performances more if told they come from of a world-renowned professional pianist rather than a conservatory student. Informing listeners that they are going to hear a professional activates reward circuitry that can persist throughout the duration of a musical excerpt. Overcoming the bias introduced by the description—choosing to prefer a performance labeled as coming from a student, for example— requires the recruitment of brain regions devoted to executive control. These findings parallel work on the impact of information about quality in other areas, for example experiments showing that people enjoy wine more if accompanied by a higher price tag. Music performance exists within a complex, multidimensional, sociocultural context, and research in the psychology of music has repeatedly demonstrated that listening is not a matter of churning out predictable responses to individual acoustic events, but rather of drawing on myriad human faculties to elicit rich, meaningful experiences. Performers are critical to this network, not just in the ways they bend and stretch the sound, but also in the ways they move in space and relate to their listeners.

The mechanics of music performance

The performance of a single piano piece might entail thousands of notes executed in precise rhythmic succession, with attributes such as loudness and inter-hand synchrony carefully controlled, sometimes at a speed of over ten notes per second, from memory, with an error rate of under 3 percent. This seems astounding. It is similarly astounding, from another perspective, that children who have had no formal training in music can sing familiar songs from memory, producing the correct pitches in the correct order for several minutes worth of notes. Both of these feats require accurate memory representations and meticulous motor control.

The circuitry behind the production of the strictly timed series of events characteristic of musical sequences can be studied by using motion capture to track finger movements, or by recording performances on instruments that have been digitally augmented to capture moment-to-moment information on key presses and other performance behaviors. One common methodology involves studying performance errors. When and where they occur can reveal information about the motor planning process.

For example, if my job is to play the notes ABCDE, and I play ABECD, it might indicate that I was already planning as far out as note E by the time I finished note B. These kinds of anticipatory errors are common in speech as well—inadvertently saying "I gave my milk the baby" instead of "I gave my baby the milk"—and indicate similar planning processes. Most studies suggest that performers plan three to four notes into the future as they play. This span increases as people gain experience; the longer someone has studied an instrument, the more anticipatory errors they make. Perhaps it can be some consolation after a botched performance that the error required elaborate training to make? Performers also systematically make more errors in the inner voices of a musical texture, rather than in the more salient top voice, which often contains the melody, or in the bottom voice, which often provides the harmonic foundation. Conveniently, these inner voice errors are the hardest for listeners to detect.

Circumstances often call on performers to play from a score they have never seen before, a skill termed sight-reading. This skill can be studied using eye-tracking technology that dynamically measures changes in the point of gaze while people perform an activity. Eye-tracking studies show that better sight-readers fixate for shorter periods of time—a quick glance is sufficient to apprehend the information at any particular moment. This speediness comes from the ability of experienced sight-readers to chunk individual notes into familiar patterns, such as chords or stereotypical melodic figures. Because of their dependence on expectations to execute movements based on partial information, good sight-readers perform better when the music stays predictably in its home key, moves by small steps, and uses conventional patterns. Although people speculate broadly about what makes a good sight reader, the single best predictor of sight-reading skill is the number of pieces the person has sight-read in the past. For a task that depends on anticipating what is going to come next, there is simply no substitute for sight-reading enough pieces that your hands can leap to likely continuations as you play.

Practice makes a difference

Research on the role of fluency in sight reading makes a compelling case for the merits of hard work—and research on the role of practice in performance makes an even stronger case. Professors at the Music Academy of West Berlin identified a group of violin students who represented the institution's very best performers and another group of violin students who were merely good. Exhaustive surveys of violinists in these two groups revealed that they were distinguished by different life experiences: violinists in the best group had accumulated more than 7,000 hours of practice by the age of eighteen, but violinists in the good group had accumulated only about 5,000 by the same age. Other research on elementary school children just beginning to play an instrument showed that success on a music performance task could be explained by a student's amount of motivation (as measured by persistence despite failure on a laboratory task) and the amount of time they practiced their instrument. No other measure, including intelligence and a general musical aptitude test, was able to predict their success. More practice has also been shown to lead to faster transitions from key to key in pianists and more consistency in expressive performance.

Research also argues for the importance of quality practice over the mere number of hours spent at the instrument. Playing through a piece repeatedly, although a tempting salvo to run out the clock for kids whose parents have set a timer for their practice session, does not qualify as effective practice. Research suggests, instead, that quality practice is deliberate, involving careful self-management, attention, goal-setting, and focus. A study of more than 10,000 twins argued that genetics affects musical ability not only directly, but also indirectly, by influencing the inclination to practice. Thus, some of the findings currently attributed to practice may ultimately prove to have their roots in biology.

When people begin practicing, they inefficiently activate wide swaths of neurons in sensorimotor areas of the brain. As they learn to play a piece, information from auditory, visual, and other centers is integrated into movement patterns that can be executed automatically. Across the course of this learning process, activity in the cortex—the seat of higher cognition—decreases and activity in movement-controlling subcortical areas like the basal ganglia and cerebellum increases. One piece of good news for people who may not be able to consistently access their instrument is that mental practice activates brain regions that are highly similar to the ones activated by actual practicing. Multiple studies show that when combined with practice on the instrument, it can be a highly effective tool. The critical auditory-motor link that underlies music performance also influences music training. Much instruction around the world involves not lectures about performance, or verbal tips, but rather simple imitation, where the teacher plays a passage and students attempt to replicate it.

No matter how much time a performer spends in a practice room, however, nothing quite prepares her for the pressure of walking out onto a stage before an expectant audience. Especially in Western classical traditions, music performance can elicit anxiety, both somatic (butterflies in the stomach, dry mouth, shallow breathing) and cognitive (negative thoughts before a performance, excessive worry). Although beta blockers have been shown to alleviate some aspects of somatic anxiety, musical performance anxiety is overall notoriously difficult to treat. Research suggests that the best strategy is to attempt to prevent it by introducing public performance into the lives of music students early, in low-stakes, low-pressure settings.

Creativity and improvisation

Performances, compositions, and improvisations can be creative to varying extents. One active line of research in psychology assumes that creativity is a stable personal characteristic—that one person might be generally more creative than another, for example. To measure creativity this research uses tasks like the Remote Association Test—in which people see three seemingly unrelated words (such as pie, luck, and belly) and must identify a fourth that relates to all of them (in this case, pot)—and fluidity assessments, in which people must list all the possible uses they can think of for a common household item. Researchers employ neuroimaging to examine the brain activity that underlies creative problem solving of this sort.

Another perspective looks at creativity as a property that emerges out of a social system, rather than a property that arises out of an individual. In this view, promulgated by psychologist Mihaly Csikszentmihalyi, creativity requires a domain characterized by discrete rules and constraints within which it is possible for a community of experts to recognize innovation. Research about music and creativity often uses jazz improvisation as this domain. Since neuroimaging shows that similar brain regions are activated when producing jazz improvisation and when producing novel, never-before-said sentences, work about musical creativity can be taken as representative of creative processes more broadly construed.

One study used neuroimaging to examine expert jazz performers as they improvised at the keyboard (thanks to a clever setup that made it possible to play inside an fMRI scanner). What emerged as most interesting was not so much which brain areas were activated during successful improvisation, but which ones were switched off. During these periods, activity in the part of the brain responsible for self-monitoring—the dorsolateral prefrontal cortex—shut down, implying that a performer needs to silence some components of executive function to create the space for novel associations to emerge.

Philosophical and scientific problems often intermingle in the psychology of music. Work on creativity is no exception. What counts as musical creativity? Is a musically creative person necessarily creative in other domains as well? Questions like these require both careful philosophical thought and rigorous experimental inquiry. Psychological work on musical creativity would benefit from closer relationships between theoretical, definitional accounts and empirical approaches to the topic. A domain as culturally embedded and complex as human creativity requires sustained engagement from multiple disciplines for headway to occur.

Although it may seem like the holy grail of psychological research on performance and improvisation to ask which expressive characteristics make a performance good, this question cannot lie entirely in the domain of psychology. A whole host of sociocultural factors may lead one person to find Beyoncé's performances moving and transformative, and another to change the station. Headlines that emerge in the popular press announcing that science has discovered the ingredients for a good song should raise suspicions. My good song might be your terrible song, and for good reason. Responsible work in the psychology of music delineates the borders of its questions and specifies the population to whom its findings might generalize. A model of music performance does not go straight from acoustic signal to listener experience; rather, it embraces at all sides the influence of the social context, ranging from what the performance looks like to where it takes place and how that relates to the listener's previous experiences. This dynamic interplay is precisely what makes music such a fascinating human endeavor, worthy of such sustained study.

Chapter 6
Human musicality

What does it mean to be musical? Some people spend all their free time going to concerts and crafting intricate playlists; others prefer talk radio. Some people apply themselves earnestly to the enterprise of learning an instrument, working through method books and diligently studying notation; others pick one up and sound out their favorite tunes, teaching themselves how to play by ear. Some people respond sensitively to music—easily finding themselves swaying along, engrossed by what they hear; others could not care less what is coming from the speakers. The fact that the ability to perform and appreciate music varies so substantially from person to person raises questions about the nature of musical capacity and how it is acquired. What kind of musicality are people born with, and how does it develop in such diverse ways?

Pitch perception

One central aspect of musicality is pitch perception. Sound waves with faster frequencies (featuring more cycles per second) are heard as "high" rather than "low"—a culturally contingent metaphor experienced as "small" versus "large" in parts of Indonesia and "weak" versus "strong" among the Bashi people in central Africa. But pitch perception can also include sensitivity to the exact frequency being played—is it a B? Is it a C?—and to the position of this note within the surrounding tonal context.

Tonality refers to the sense that pitches are heard in relation to a central, governing tonic. If I sang a tune in the key of C—where C functions as this central tonic—the pitch B would sound unstable, conveying a sense that it should resolve up to C. If I sang a tune in the key of B, however, that same pitch B could now be heard as highly stable, not implying any need for resolution—in fact, it could now serve quite convincingly as the final note of the song.

In a classic experiment, Cornell psychologist Carol Krumhansl played listeners brief tonal contexts, such as a scale or chord progression, followed by a single probe tone. After each probe, she asked a simple question: how well did it fit with the preceding context? She created tone profiles out of the responses. These profiles plot probes along the x-axis and goodness-of-fit ratings along the y-axis. If the probes are listed in order starting with the tonic of the prevailing context, the profiles look more or less the same in every key. People hear the tonic as fitting the context best, and out-of-key notes as fitting worst. Their responses reveal that pitch relationally: the experience of any individual note is shaped by its position within the governing tonal schema.

Later, researchers discovered that simply by counting up the number of times each pitch occurred in music in a particular key, they could produce plots remarkably similar to the tone profiles. The pitch B occurred much more frequently in the key of B, for example, than in the key of C. The similarity between the frequency-of-occurrence plots and the goodness-of-fit plots made it possible to believe that the implicit tracking of statistics about note frequency helps give rise to perceptions of tonality.

The ability to abstract beyond specific pitches and hear in relation to a central tonic is called relative pitch. Relational perceptions of

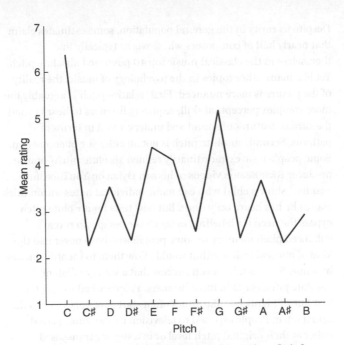

7. This chart plots goodness-of-fit ratings on the y-axis and pitches on the x-axis. Called a tone profile, it looks the same for every major key, so long as the x-axis is ordered starting at the first note of the scale. Charts that plot the frequency of occurrence of each note in pieces written in the key also look strikingly similar, suggesting that tracking the statistics about what tends to happen in music feeds into perceptions of key.

this sort dominate most people's sense of pitch, but for some people (with estimates ranging from as few as 1 in 10,000 to as many as 1 in 100), absolute pitch—the identity of the actual note being played, regardless of context—is more salient. To these listeners, the C-ness of C is more noticeable than how it functions within the surrounding tonal context.

People with absolute pitch can hear the hum of a vacuum cleaner and identify it as an F-sharp. This ability can seem prodigious.

Despite its rarity in the general population, some estimates claim that nearly half of composers whose works typically find themselves in the classical music top 40 possessed absolute pitch. Yet like many other topics in the psychology of music, the reality of the picture is more nuanced. First, relative pitch is arguably the more complex perceptual skill, requiring listeners to hear beyond the surface features of sound and understand it in terms of patterns. Second, absolute pitch is not an either/or phenomenon. Some people have extraordinarily refined absolute pitch—music producer Rick Beato's videos of his son Dylan on YouTube, for example, show a child who can name individual notes within thick chords he has heard only once. But new tests for absolute pitch bypass the need for labeling, using clever designs to reveal enhanced pitch memory in some people who have never had the kind of musical training that would allow them to identify pitches by name. Some studies even suggest that a variety of latent absolute pitch exists in most listeners. People asked to sing the first line of highly familiar tunes often start at or very close to the actual pitch. People exposed to television theme songs played either at their original pitch level or in a slightly transposed version are good at detecting which was the original version featured in the show. Although most people could not sing a C if you asked them, they might be able to perform the functional equivalent simply by singing the first note of the theme song from *The Simpsons*.

Another way of thinking about the spectrum of pitch perception is to assume that all these ways of hearing are perceptually available to some extent. Exposure to typical musical practices across the span of development encourages the application of various filters, as children come to learn that certain aspects of sound are more musically relevant than others. Whereas they start out describing melodies in terms of pitch height, as they get a little older they start focusing on the melodies' contours—how they move up or down. Eventually, they focus more on relationships with a central tonic.

The development of musicality

To understand how basic elements of musicality such as pitch perception emerge and how they vary from person to person, it can be helpful to examine the stages of development across which people acquire musical skills. No prospect offers quite so much potential as the notion of studying infants as if they were musical blank slates, capable of defining the contours of their musical capacity before it is influenced by culture and experience. But infants have already been exposed to a complex soundscape in utero, ranging from the regular pulses of the mother's heartbeat to voices and music in the surrounding environment. Newborns not only recognize their mother's voice, but also melodies they heard frequently while in the womb. The sounds to which they have been exposed before birth shape infant musicality—thus no musical blank slate exists.

Music intrigues infants. Parents can provide firsthand reports of the transfixed stare with which many babies respond to music, and numerous studies have shown that singing to babies reduces fussing. Infants' perceptual systems allow them to abstract substantial information about their musical surroundings. Six-month-old infants listen longer to music when pauses occur in their typical location between phrases rather than at random midphrase moments—they know, to a certain extent, how the music should go.

But they are also remarkably malleable and able to adapt to different musical systems. Although a preference for the consonant intervals many adults identify as pleasant has been detected in infants as young as two months old, other studies show that so long as the music is not familiar, six-month-old babies do not particularly care whether a song uses consonant or dissonant intervals. Among adults, a preference for consonance is widespread, but not universal. Some Croatian folk singers in rural regions accompany one another using parallel seconds, considered by many Western traditions one of the most dissonant intervals. The Tsimane', a native Amazonian tribe with little exposure to Western culture, rate consonant and dissonant intervals as equally pleasant. Although Western adults detect changes to melodies much better when they are composed using Western scales, infants are equally good at detecting changes to melodies composed using Western scales or the Javanese pelog scale or an artificial invented scale—so long as it retains the property of dividing the octave into unequal scale steps, as do most scale systems around the world.

Baby minds are equally plastic when it comes to musical timing. Psychologists Erin Hannon and Sandra Trehub assessed this versatility using two types of meter. One type, prevalent in much of the West, is isochronous—the same amount of time separates one beat from the next—and the other, common in the folk music of the Balkans, is nonisochronous—the distance between beats alternates between a shorter and a longer duration. Western six-month-old infants can detect changes just as easily in isochronous as nonisochronous meters, but Western adults are incapable of detecting changes in the unfamiliar nonisochronous meters.

Between six and twelve months of age, babies' immersion in their own musical culture continues, and the perceptual system starts to prune itself, reallocating unused perceptual capacities to permit more specialization in the sound structures they encounter most frequently. Accordingly, when Western twelve-month-olds are tested on the same task, they demonstrate an adult-like inability to detect changes in nonisochronous meters.

Yet the story is a little more complicated. Parents of these twelve-month-olds were provided a ten-minute CD of Balkan folk music and instructed to play it for the babies twice a day over a two-week period. When retested at the end of this time, the twelve-month-olds were once more able to detect changes in both the isochronous and the nonisochronous meters. Short-term, passive exposure was sufficient for them to regain the perceptual skills necessary for handling nonisochronous meters. Western adults, on the other hand, even after they had diligently listened to the same CD for a week or two, remained unable to detect changes in nonisochronous meters.

Infancy seems to present a special window of musical plasticity. Just as babies can learn whatever language they are exposed to, they adapt to whatever musical system surrounds them. And just as adults have a harder time learning a new language once the window of plasticity has passed, they also have a harder time adjusting to a new musical system. Ironically, parents looking for a take-home lesson from research about music psychology might conclude not that it is beneficial to play your baby Mozart all day, as popular conceptions of the field might suggest, but rather that exposure to a wide range of musical styles might best take advantage of the infant mind's capacity to absorb different musical systems.

Other areas of musical competence emerge over the developmental span, with more universal musical attributes, such as rhythm, generally learned earlier, and musical attributes that appear in fewer of the world's musical systems, such as harmony, generally learned later. This pattern would be expected if more of the universal musical attributes took the best advantage of the constraints and affordances of the perceptual system—the developing mind would then tune into these characteristics earlier and more easily. But it is almost impossible to tease out the possible role of perceptual constraints from the myriad political and historical factors that influence the degree of universality in musical practices.

Consistent with the trajectory predicted if perceptual limitations were relevant, children develop sensitivity to key before they develop sensitivity to harmony. It is common for musical cultures around the world to feature a central pitch and scale that together might be thought of as constituting a key, but rarer for them to feature the kind of harmonic structures (such as rules governing chords or the way pitches sound when played together) that are characteristic of Western music. When exposed to excerpts that flagrantly end in the wrong key, Western four-year-olds think they sound just as good as excerpts that end in the right key. Five-year-olds, however, consistently rate them as worse. When singing, young children tend to wander from one key to another while preserving the contour (they move up or down when appropriate, but by a different amount than mandated by the key). Sensitivity to harmony and the chords implied by conventional melodies does not generally develop until closer to the age of eight.

The ability to synchronize with a beat appears even earlier than the ability to represent key and harmony. Toddlers often dance along to music, but their body movements do not consistently align with the beat until the preschool years. Studies that asked children to tap along to recorded music suggested that synchronization does not happen reliably until age four, but subsequent studies that asked children to drum along with a human partner rather than tap to a recording revealed that two-and-a-half- year-old children actually can synchronize. The discrepancy between children's synchronization success with recordings versus human partners underscores the importance of using tasks that are realistic, socially embedded, and sufficiently motivating to elicit top performance. Some people attribute the divergent findings not to a difference in the tasks presented, but to a difference in the statistics and mathematics used to model synchronization. This controversy points to the importance of all aspects of a study's design in determining the conclusions that can be drawn from it.

Similar constraints hold for studies about the capacity of young children to experience music emotionally. Laboratory studies that systematically vary musical features and ask children to label the emotion being expressed demonstrate that preschoolers (ages three to four) can associate tempo and loudness with emotion labels similar to the ones adults provide. Not until children are closer to the age of six to eight, however, can they associate changes in mode (switching from minor to major) with conventional emotion labels. But neither the experience of listening to music in a laboratory nor of selecting a specific emotion label reflects the ways children ordinarily interact with music. Children exhibit appropriate responses to lullabies, for example, well before the age of three or four. The capacity of slow, quiet music to soothe them might easily be thought about as a kind of emotional response. Similarly, young children situated in natural social environments and given the kinds of contextual cues normally present when listening to music—even if they are unable to label emotional associations explicitly—might show facial expressions that indicate a more nuanced appreciation of music's expressive character than studies have captured to date.

The effects of musical training

The notion of musical training spans all kinds of experiences, from formal violin lessons and theory classes to learning the guitar by ear, playing in a drum circle, or attending concerts. But the first kind—formal training in the classical tradition—is the one that has been best studied, partly because it is the tradition out of which many psychologists of music emerged, partly because it is a discrete and well-defined endeavor, and partly because it involves a set of demanding, time-consuming physical and mental activities that make it likely to generate measurable cognitive changes in contrast to a control group that does not undertake them.

Studies investigating formal musical training often confront the challenge of disentangling the effects of the training itself from the effects of being the sort of person who seeks out musical training, sticks with it, and has access to it in the first place. Most experiments work by randomly assigning participants to a particular treatment group, to avoid selection bias. But it would not be ethical (let alone practical) to randomly assign some babies to a group that received music lessons over the first ten years of life and other babies to a group that was expressly not permitted to receive them.

Instead, researchers often try to form two groups composed of children who are matched on the characteristics likeliest to be relevant. In a typical study, they take two groups of children with comparable socioeconomic characteristics, baseline IQ scores, and personality types and provide one group with music lessons and another with some kind of control activity. (This control activity turns out to be important, since focused time with an adult instructor can have a positive impact, independent of any musical component to the interaction.) But even when controlling for participant characteristics and even when selecting a good control activity, it is possible that some unknown third factor not controlled for between the groups is driving the effect, or that some aspect of the music lesson other than its particularly musical content is responsible for any differences.

Studies—albeit ones that suffer from these limitations—have tended to find that music lessons can result in improvements on several nonmusical tasks, ranging from auditory working memory and executive functioning to reading comprehension, IQ, and school performance. The strongest body of evidence supports the impact of music training on speech perception. People who have had musical training are better at hearing speech in a noisy environment, at determining whether two sentences in a foreign language are the same or different, and at intuiting a speaker's emotion purely from the prosody (the speech melody left over when the actual phonemic content is blurred so that the words are no longer distinct). Children with musical training show better phonological awareness—the ability to focus on and manipulate the sound units that form the basis of a language. These reported effects on speech perception are further supported by clear theory about the mechanisms that underlie them. Work in Nina Kraus's lab at Northwestern University has demonstrated that neurons in the brainstem track pitch more accurately in people with musical training. It is easy to imagine how more faithful representations of pitch might enhance phonological awareness, which, in turn, influences reading skills.

Music has often been studied from the perspective of mathematics—generating quantitative models of pitch and timing, for example. Stretching back to Pythagoras, quasi-mystical notions about the relationship between music and numbers have held sway over many an imagination, prompting a significant body of research aimed at identifying the impact of musical training on mathematical ability. Yet all this work has produced little evidence that formal lessons in music affect mathematical acumen. Similarly, despite numerous studies, little evidence exists that musical training affects emotional intelligence.

Individual differences

Although much of the early work on the effect of musical training contrasted a group termed "musicians" with a group termed "nonmusicians," these terms do not seem ideal. By "musician," most of these studies meant "person with formal training in the Western classical tradition." "Nonmusician" simply meant someone without such training. These categories obscured the fact that many people labeled "nonmusicians" engage deeply with music in other ways—stewarding elaborate record collections, for example, teaching themselves everything there is to know about ska, or actually earning money as a music professional, for instance as a music critic or DJ.

Individual differences in musical abilities and behaviors extend far beyond the categories of formal training (or the lack thereof). The psychology of music is likely to progress only by contrasting other kinds of difference—between people trained by ear and people trained with notation, for example, or between people who listen voraciously and people who do not seek out musical experiences.

Since 2010, researchers have begun developing tools for characterizing these individual differences with finer resolution. The Absorption in Music Scale (AIMS) scores individuals on their general susceptibility to being captivated by listening to music by measuring their agreement with such statements as, "I will stop everything that I'm doing in order to listen to a special song/piece of music that is playing," and "Sometimes when listening to music I feel as if my mind can understand the whole world." An individual's AIMS score has been shown to predict the intensity of their emotional response to music and their tendency to imagine narratives while listening.

The Goldsmiths Musical Sophistication Index (Gold-MSI) uses a similar self-report inventory, supplemented by a battery of listening tests, to assess individual differences in musical sophistication in ways that move beyond whether a person has been formally trained. The Gold-MSI includes questions about the extent of time and resources the individual commits to music; self-report assessments about perceptual abilities, as well as listening tests that assess musical memory, beat perception, synchronization, and the capacity to detect changes in sound; musical training; singing ability; and the capacity for engaging emotionally with music. In a paper provocatively titled "The Musicality of Non-Musicians," psychologist Daniel Müllensiefen and colleagues use the Gold-MSI to demonstrate the vast range of musical behaviors and aptitudes that differentiate people without formal training.

The history of psychology's treatment of individual differences in musicality reveals the degree to which studies that might appear objective and purely scientific have their origin in cultural conceptions of music. If formal training in playing an instrument were not prioritized as a litmus test for musicianship, we might have seen a bevy of studies investigating the effects of avid musical listening rather than the effects of practicing an instrument. The behaviors and dispositions that get encoded into variables and studied are dependent on society's conceptions and valuations of them. For this reason, the psychology of music cannot proceed without the deep involvement of humanists. It is imperative to think deeply about the ways that musical ideas, practices, and assumptions affect the topics and variables music psychologists study and the ways that findings in the psychology of music are interpreted and understood.

Special musical abilities

The extreme ends of the spectrum of individual differences in music make especially interesting cases. Musical prodigies, who attain startling mastery at a young age, can challenge assumptions about the workings of the musical mind. Born in 2005, Alma Deutscher had composed a full-length violin concerto and a full-length opera by the age of ten, calling to mind that most famous of child prodigies, Wolfgang Amadeus Mozart, born 250 years earlier, who wrote his first symphony at the age of seven.

Deutscher and Mozart share the capacity for absolute pitch, early exposure to music through a parent who is an avid musician, early training in composition and improvisation, the early accumulation of many hours devoted to music (Deutscher is homeschooled), and an apparently genuine delight in music making. Aside from the astounding perceptual, cognitive, executive, and motor skills required to compose or perform lengthy, sophisticated music as a child, the ability to create expressively convincing music seems particularly challenging to ordinary conceptions of how music works. If music articulates some of the subtlest and most difficult to express layers of emotional experience, how can children compose moving passages without the benefit of decades of ecstasies and disappointments? Prodigies do not readily emerge in fields like poetry that rely on this kind of maturity.

Musical savants—individuals with low cognitive functioning who can nevertheless perform the kind of musical feats that would seem to belie their other disabilities—exhibit a different but equally stunning kind of musical aptitude. Pianists Rex Lewis-Clack and Derek Paravicini are blind and share serious cognitive disabilities that make every day functioning difficult, yet they also possess an extremely accurate sense for absolute pitch and the kind of musical ability that enables them not just to play the piano, but also to improvise, and to hear a song once and play it back as if they had studied it for years. Some researchers have suggested that speech and vision deficits might permit more brain areas to be co-opted for auditory processing. Moreover, in the absence of other kinds of stimuli, savants may spend a truly unusual amount of time at an instrument from a very young age. Videos online show Rex Lewis-Clack as a toddler, falling asleep next to his keyboard, one little arm resisting oblivion by continuing to grasp at the keys.

One genetic developmental disorder, Williams syndrome, tends to involve low IQ, learning difficulties, and problems with math and spatial reasoning, but carries with it heightened performance in language and music, as well as an exuberant, extroverted orientation to other people. Children with Williams syndrome are often highly interested in music, and especially sensitive to its emotional content.

The appearance of these streaks of musical ability in unexpected places—emerging at a young age or alongside other kinds of deficits—provides opportunities for understanding the limits and potential of the musical mind. It also serves as a reminder that musicality encompasses a range of different behaviors and attitudes. The autistic child who can name all the notes in a thirteen-voice chord yet plays with little expressive inflection is tapping into a different part of musicality than the child with Williams syndrome who finds herself tearing up in response to a Schubert song.

Special musical deficits

People are more likely to complain that they suffer from a musical deficit than brag that they are gifted with a special musical ability. More than 15 percent of the population alleges that they are tone deaf, even though the most liberal definition of amusia—a clinical disorder affecting pitch processing—implicates less than 5 percent of the population.

What accounts for the overly pessimistic self-diagnoses? On the one hand, Western culture relegates music performance to the domain of specialists more so than most cultures around the world. Outside the Western classical tradition, it is more common for music making to involve everyone as participants, rather than to divide the performer and the audience into separate groups. People's tendency to disavow their own musical competence might stem from this fetishization of the professional. On the other hand, people may refer to themselves as tone deaf not when they have a problem perceiving pitch, but when they have a problem producing it—when they feel they "can't hold a tune." Poor singing can arise from problems with motor planning that do not relate to pitch perception at all.

The clinical test for amusia involves listening to pairs of melodies, some of which include a change to one pitch that ordinary listeners find egregious. Tasked with saying whether the melodies are the same or different, amusics find themselves unable to answer correctly. Intriguingly, this deficit in fine-grained pitch perception occurs separately from aphasia, a speech processing disorder. People with amusia can generally understand the prosodic aspects of language just fine—they know when a sentence is serving as a question or expressing disapproval, for example. Yet when the speech sounds are blurred out, leaving only the melody of the utterance, amusics struggle. This contrast suggests that they probably rely on parallel information streams outside of pitch to function in real-world speech contexts. Although the consequences for speech perception are minimal, their struggle with pitch processing does have other important consequences. It affects broader cognitive abilities such as musical memory, and can have powerful social effects, as people with amusia fail to recognize familiar tunes or rely on friends' facial expressions to know whether a wrong note was played or not.

Although amusia can result in diminished musical enjoyment, musical anhedonia—a general failure to derive pleasure from music—also occurs independent of any problem with pitch processing. People with musical anhedonia perceive music normally, and possess intact, undamaged reward circuitry. They are able to derive pleasure from other activities, but find themselves incapable of being moved or pleased by music. They do not show typical physiological responses to it, and report a general lack of musical interest—they do not create playlists in Spotify or listen to the radio. Recent neuroimaging work showed that people who are especially passionate about music possess greater connectivity between the auditory cortex and the subcortical reward network, whereas people with musical anhedonia show reduced connectivity between these regions. In other words, people unable to derive pleasure from music, although they have perfectly competent sound processing centers and pleasure centers, may lack the linkage between the two regions that would enable feeling thrilled by music.

Chapter 7
The appetite for music

Music can seem captivating and integral to our lives, yet these affective dimensions are precisely the ones for which understanding remains most elusive. It is relatively straightforward to study something like musical memory by manipulating excerpts in various situations and testing whether people remember them; studying the way music moves us requires deeper thought. It also represents a unique opportunity for the psychology of music.

The challenge of characterizing the engrossing, moving, and emotional aspects of musical experience extends beyond psychology; musicology and philosophy have struggled to find adequate concepts for framing them, just as everyday listeners can struggle to describe a powerful experience they had at a concert. Music psychology's general approach to this problem might seem disappointing—studies often manipulate individual aspects of the musical experience and measure some unsatisfactory proxy for emotional response. For example, a typical study might alter some musical feature, like whether a piece is in a major or a minor key, or whether the listener heard it in a room filled with other people or in isolation, and ask participants to rate how happy or sad the excerpt seemed on a scale from 1 to 7. Clearly, the primary factors that conspire to generate deep musical experiences are not modality (whether a piece is in major or minor) or the presence or absence of other listeners, and the primary characteristic of a deep musical experience is not identifying a piece as happy or sad. But it is precisely the way that these studies offer small, incomplete, and yet tractable nuggets of insight that can propel them into a dialogue that drives understanding forward. When a philosopher seeking to illuminate musical experience encounters a study like this, she can use it to carve into negative space that is otherwise difficult to explore. By pushing back against the notion that a deep musical experience can be assayed by asking about happy and sad labels, she provides grist to her own arguments—which then can spark psychologists to do additional studies, which, in turn, inspire even more finely hewn theories from the philosopher, and so on until a seemingly insurmountable problem has been solved by working it, incrementally, from both ends.

Emotional responses to music

Not all difficult-to-articulate musical experiences are emotional. A person might find herself gripped by a piece of music—alert, attentive, and interested—without experiencing an emotion per se. But for many people, music's capacity to reach inside of them and coax out complex, real emotions is an important part of its place in their lives.

It is important to distinguish between two kinds of experiences. On the one hand, music can evoke emotion. Listening to a song can lead a person to weep in sorrow or to experience great joy. But sometimes, rather than actually experiencing an emotional state, listening to a song might lead a person merely to recognize that the music is *expressive of* sorrow or joy. Although both of these responses are interesting, the first has received more attention from music psychology because it is so puzzling. Emotions are usually inspired by clear events relevant to a person's goals. For example, sorrow might be elicited by the prospect of abandonment and joy by the hope of reconciliation. Music

8. A child has a strong emotional response while listening to *Peter and the Wolf*.

cannot abandon someone or reconcile with them. It seems to carry no goal-relevant object that would render it capable of triggering an emotional response.

This fundamental mystery has inspired an effort to specify the mechanisms through which music might elicit emotion, an effort summarized concisely by Swedish psychologists Patrik Juslin and Daniel Västfjäll. Most basically, sounds that are sudden, loud, or unpleasant can trigger a brainstem reflex meant to modulate arousal in response to events that could pose an imminent threat. Even though a listener may well be aware that a loud chord presents no danger, this hardwired system works pre-attentively, readying a person to respond even in situations that might ultimately prove innocuous—similar to the way a stray stick spotted by a runner can evoke a startle response before slower, more reasoned cognitive systems intervene to register that it is not a snake.

Aside from harnessing primitive neural systems to signal peril, music can conjure up the kind of real-world association—not of itself musical—that might elicit emotion via evaluative conditioning and episodic memory. Songs played around a campfire every summer during a person's teenage years can elicit powerful nostalgia years later. Casually overhearing a tune that figured prominently in a past relationship can bring all the emotions associated with that person flooding back. In these cases, the object of the emotion is not the music itself, so much as the real-life person or event it conjures up. Because of this extramusical source, music psychologists have tended to be less interested in the evaluative conditioning mechanism for musical emotions, thinking that the music itself plays only a peripheral role. But this assumption overlooks two intriguing aspects worthy of further study.

First, how does sound so easily take on such powerful associations with the life circumstances in which it was encountered? Recent work shows that music evokes more vivid autobiographical memories than familiar faces. When University of California at Davis psychologist Petr Janata played people chart-topping songs from their adolescence, they reported associating specific autobiographical memories with most of the familiar songs. Neuroimaging showed that the act of listening to popular songs from their teenage years and recalling associated memories depended on activity in the medial prefrontal cortex, a region whose functioning tends to be preserved even late into the progression of Alzheimer's disease. This region's centrality in the music-memory link may help explain why playing music from the adolescence of a person with Alzheimer's can sometimes elicit improved memory and attention in these patients.

Second, how does music amplify the emotions elicited by these associations to create a special, high-arousal state in which the emotions manifest themselves even more powerfully than they might in other circumstances? My own favorite example of this comes from junior high and high school summers spent at Interlochen, an eight-week music camp in Michigan where the final night was always marked by a performance of Liszt's *Les Preludes*, after which the conductor broke the baton to signal the end of that year's session. All the campers used to spend the performance huddled together, weeping at the prospect of leaving. For several decades, well past the point when thinking explicitly about Interlochen could conjure up any nostalgia, the emergence of its distinctive theme, unbidden on the radio, could still trigger chills and tears. When overt thoughts about adolescent summers elicit only shrugs, but oblique associations raised by music elicit full-blown emotions, the music is clearly contributing more than merely pointing to a life experience.

In addition to brainstem reflexes and evaluative conditioning, a third mechanism proposed by Juslin and Västfjäll is emotional contagion. When people see faces expressive of a particular emotion, their own facial muscles often contort themselves involuntarily into a subtle sympathetic mirror. When they hear voices expressive of a particular emotion (low, slow, and punctuated by pauses, for example), they imagine their own voice moving this way, potentially inducing the associated underlying state (sadness). The discovery of mirror neurons in the monkey premotor cortex—neurons that fire not only when the animal performs an action, but also when it sees or hears someone else do it—bolsters the hypothesis that a brain network exists to support translating perceived human action into imagined or performed human action. Music may take advantage of this system by creating sounds that exaggerate the characteristics of the expressive voice—playing lower and slower than a human could speak, for example—inducing an especially charged emotional state.

Music may also elicit emotions by triggering visual imagery. People generate visual imagery and imagined stories easily in response to music. In a recent study, almost 60 percent of people presented with excerpts of orchestral music reported imagining a story or elements of a story. These images and stories can, in turn, elicit emotion. Like evaluative conditioning, this mechanism relies on music's capacity to conjure up extramusical associations that can serve as triggers for emotional response. It raises a host of important research questions. How do these associations emerge? Do they stem from an inherent tendency to understand abstract domains in terms of images and stories or do particular cultural experiences encourage listeners to hear music this way? What role does film's pervasive pairing of music and imagery play in shaping this response? When listeners experience an extramusical association, to what degree does the association tend to be visual?

Most of these mechanisms rely on music's entanglement with nonmusical entities—the way music can reference particular experiences or objects or social groups. However, one mechanism—musical expectancy—depends more exclusively on the purely sonic aspects. This theory, first developed by Leonard Meyer in the 1950s, links moments of musical surprise with experiences of emotion and expressivity. Even listeners without formal training anticipate particular continuations as the music progresses. By deviating from these expectations—leaping to a far-away note or stepping out of the key—music can generate tension and expressive intensity.

Emotional responses to music can range from a momentary sense of poignancy to a powerful and long-lasting transformative state. About 50 percent of people say that they have experienced chills while listening to music. Chills involve a pleasurable sense of shivers down the spine or tingling. Goosebumps spread across the torso and arm hairs stand on end. People prone to musical chills do not tend to be drawn to roller coasters or skydiving or extreme sports. It seems that for some, a change of key suffices to generate a sense of ecstatic transport, while others might need to jump out of a plane.

Although Beethoven might trigger chills reliably for one listener and Elvis for another, the chills-inducing moments tend to share certain characteristics. Most often, they involve a sudden change from soft to loud or from one key to another, or the addition of a new instrument, or a sudden shift in range (from low to high or vice versa). Neuroimaging studies show that musical chills depend on the brain regions that underlie other euphoric experiences.

Euphoric may seem like a strong descriptor, but people can sustain truly ecstatic experiences of music. In the 1960s, psychologist Abraham Maslow studied peak experiences—rare, quasi-mystical sensations of bliss that lead the person sustaining them to feel they are perceiving reality in an exhilarating new way—and concluded that music and sex were the easiest shortcuts to them. Forty years later, Alf Gabrielsson took up this music-ecstasy connection and asked more than a thousand people to freely describe the strongest experience they had ever had with music. The occasional enjoyment of peak musical experiences was not restricted to certain demographics or personality types or to certain genres of music, although more flexible and open people tended to be more prone to them. During peak listening episodes, people often report heightened emotionality, along with a sense that their body's borders have dissolved and merged into the music, and a perception that they have gained new and important insight.

Although peak experiences are rare, the memory of them tends to linger and shape the way people think about themselves and their world. Because of their substantial influence, a question arises about the degree to which ordinary experiences of music function as paler versions of peak episodes or rather as something entirely different in kind. Work examining people's proclivity to listen and relisten to the same songs suggests that one of the things this repetition achieves is to fold listeners into the music, absorbing them in an almost participatory way. Because relistening allows them to predict what is coming next, and to internally imagine that continuation before it occurs, familiar music can wrap listeners into its course, generating a pleasurable sense of merging with the sound that seems related to the dissolution people describe during peak experiences. This connection suggests that ordinary and extreme musical pleasures might differ more in degree than in kind.

Aesthetic responses to music

The term "aesthetics" carries multiple meanings, and can refer to Western—especially Germanic—notions about the contemplation of beauty in art. But music psychologists tend to use it more broadly to refer to any music-driven experience, especially those residual aspects left over when the cognitive and emotional attributes are already explained. This leaves aesthetics to contend with the aspects of music that are most difficult to put into words.

When people do not even know how to talk about the experience they are attempting to study scientifically, the prospects for satisfactory insight might seem dim. But many empirical methods, it turns out, aim precisely to expose mental processes to which people lack direct access. Measuring people's reaction times in responding to some arbitrary question about a note (whether it was in tune or played by a trumpet or a violin) can illuminate the degree to which people anticipated it, even when they are utterly unable to verbalize the anticipation—even when they are oblivious to the fact that they are sustaining anticipations about notes at all.

If some aspects of aesthetic experience might be considered a dark room, hard to feel out and explore, these kinds of studies can be understood to offer a flashlight, illuminating a narrow slice that might reveal or obscure the broader characteristics depending on where it shines. In either case, they provide a way in for people seeking to understand more about what musical listening is really like—something tractable to pursue or push against.

Researchers in the burgeoning area of neuroaesthetics use fMRI to look at the areas of the brain that engage when people undergo an aesthetic experience. Then, by examining other tasks that rely on activation in these areas, they draft hypotheses about the nature and scope of aesthetic listening. Several studies implicate the orbitofrontal cortex in aesthetic processing. This region also helps encode the expected reward or punishment associated with various actions, and plays a part in the development of addictive behavior. Just because an area is active while performing two separate tasks does not mean that the tasks share fundamental attributes, but it provides a starting hypothesis. This neuroimaging work might be taken to suggest that much aesthetic experience relies less on the cool, distanced contemplation of abstract forms and more on highly self-relevant assessments, such as the question of what social group the music represents and how the listener relates to it. By working from such specific and provocative starting positions, empirical approaches can inspire richer theorizing about aesthetic experience.

Musical liking

Even people who hesitate to talk much about music can often confidently list examples of music they like and music they do not. Studies frequently seek to understand these preferences by manipulating characteristics of the music or the context within which it is experienced and asking people how much they liked it. Other work varies something about the music—such as how frequently a new part enters—and measures how long people listen to before moving on it, taking listening time as an implicit measure of preference.

Again and again, these studies reinforce the notion that people prefer music that occupies a sweet spot of complexity—music that is neither too simple nor too complex. Named after psychologist Wilhelm Wundt who first proposed it in 1874, the Wundt curve shown in Figure 9 displays this tendency. The vertical axis designates preference, liking, or enjoyment. The horizontal axis can represent familiarity or complexity. Habits of radio play exemplify the curve's trajectory. The first few times the radio plays a song, people might wait through it impatiently, hoping one of their favorites will air next. But as the station works it into its top 40 song cycle, playing it again and again, people tend to find themselves enjoying it more and more, until the arrival of some peak point—represented by the top of the inverted U—after which they start to get increasingly sick of the song, liking it less and less until it eventually rotates out of radio play.

Although the basic shape of this curve tends to capture a broad range of musical experiences, neither the slope of the sides nor the height of the peak are fixed. Personality plays a role—people high in an attribute referred to as "openness to new experience"

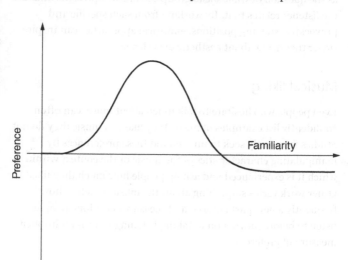

9. This inverted-U-shaped curve traces the way people initially tend to like a song more as they hear it more. Past a certain point, however, they tend to like it less with increasing exposure, sometimes ultimately liking it even less than on the first hearing.

generally prefer more complex music, shifting their preference curve to the right relevant to other listeners. People who score high on the Absorption in Music Scale may regularly sustain higher peak enjoyment experiences than other listeners, stretching their preference curve upward.

Not only does personality influence the route through the inverted U, but so does the lifetime of musical experiences a person brings to the listening episode. A King Crimson song might sound alienatingly complex to someone new to the genre, but immediately digestible to a devoted fan of progressive rock. Because it sounds complex to one listener and simple to another, preferences for the same song can start out at different points on the inverted U even for listeners with much in common.

The lifetime set of a person's previous musical experiences and that person's personality are not wholly independent variables, because personality influences genre preference. People high on openness to new experience tend to prefer genres they view as more complex, such as classical, jazz, and metal. Extroverts tend to prefer conventional genres such as pop, especially when the music is fast and danceable. Moreover, people's preferences tend to solidify during adolescence, the period when they listen to the most music and when this listening seems especially relevant to the definition of their burgeoning identity. Adults asked later in life about different songs tend to prefer the ones that were commonly played during their adolescence, as well as the ones that were played during their parents' adolescence. Presumably, the parents' lingering penchant for the music of their own teenage years translated into playing it more around the house, disproportionally exposing their children to these songs and simultaneously shaping the preferences of a new generation.

People often wonder if music psychologists could devise a formula to help write hit songs. But musical preferences depend on highly dynamic processes. Enjoyment of a song arises not just out of its intrinsic characteristics, but also out of prior exposure, familiarity with similar songs, personality, and stage in life. As if that were not sufficient evidence for the implausibility of a formula, numerous other studies document the role of factors far outside the border of the notes in determining preference.

Listeners exposed to brief excerpts from string quartets liked them less when they had read a description of the excerpt beforehand. Although learning more about a piece might eventually lead to richer experiences, it can apparently also lead to a short-term deficit. Integrating musical sound with verbal information might seem strenuous, and therefore unpleasant. Descriptions might also encourage listeners to adopt a more objective, reflective stance—a position diametrically opposed to the kind of imagined participation often shown to be a component of highly pleasurable musical experiences. Sustained study may allow listeners to integrate the knowledge more effortlessly, experiencing the music in terms of its insights without the intervention of this thoughtful distancing.

The presentation of information has wide-ranging effects beyond just preference. Listeners thought orchestral excerpts were more moving when told that the composer wrote them for some happy reason (to celebrate a friend's arrival, for example) than when told they wrote them for a neutral or unhappy reason (such as mourning a friend's loss). Listeners who were told that musical passages had come from a soundtrack accompanying a sad or a neutral film scene thought the passages themselves sounded sadder. Musical experience and musical preference depend on the complex interplay not only of the characteristics of the sound itself, but also of the predilections and prior experiences of the listener, as well as the setting and context within which each piece is heard.

Musical functions and motivation

Given music's ubiquity in human culture, it is reasonable to ask what drives people's interest in it. Yet the variety of music's uses—

ranging from facilitating contemplation at a concert hall to encouraging community bonding at a church to pumping up exercisers at the gym—argues against a single motivation and in favor of a taxonomy of different ones. To start envisioning what this taxonomy might be like, it helps to think in terms of what kinds of experience music affords or makes possible. Six basic candidates for these categories might include movement, play, communication, social bonding, emotion, and identity.

Music's capacity to spur movement—especially coordinated movement—underlies not only its use in dance, but also during exercise, in various rehabilitative contexts such as therapies for Parkinson's disease, and during synchronized work efforts like farming or rowing. This capacity was known well before neuroimaging revealed motor activation during music listening; the medieval church, disdaining the earthly, prescribed a type of chant that eschewed the kind of temporal regularity that engages the body. On the other side, athletic wear companies have devised apps and playlists that tailor music to a user's desired running pace.

Music also can serve broadly as play. Shepherds invent songs to pass the time; aficionados of complex art music prioritize aesthetic contemplation. Music can capture attention from a solitary listener or facilitate interaction between participants, as in a campfire jam or singalong. Some people have even theorized that music's facilitation of play formed an important part of its evolutionary history—by engaging people in safe time-passing, it prevented mischief and dangers.

People also turn to music for its ability to communicate. The Mbuti of the Congo region use song to convey locational information across large distances, and residents of La Gomera, one of the Canary Islands, have traditionally used a whistled version of Spanish to communicate across the steep island landscape. Following in the footsteps of Richard Wagner, who used musical leitmotivs to denote characters, objects, and ideas in his operas, the *Star Wars* movies employ passages like the Death Star theme not only to conjure up a certain emotional register, but also quite literally to refer to the Death Star.

One of music's central functions, also prominent in theories about its evolutionary origins, is social bonding. Music plays an important role in rituals and ceremonies the world over, and can conjure a sense of communion among two people sharing an intimate jazz performance or a hundred thousand people attending an event. Its ability to encourage joint attending in time seems critical to the sense of sharing and connection it can elicit.

Music can also choreograph emotions in wide-ranging ways. People turn to it so commonly to regulate their own moods that playlists devoted to this purpose have begun cropping up on Spotify and other streaming music services: "music to help you survive a breakup" or "music to inflate your confidence before an important meeting." Music is especially good at both sparking and absorbing the surfeit of emotions that can arise in very fraught circumstances. Film and television regularly rely on this capacity. Multiple studies show that switching out the music accompanying such innocuous visual scenes as a car traversing a road can lead people to view the situation as ominous, cheerful, or tragic for the car's inhabitants.

Finally, music can serve to generate, define, or alter individual and group identities. This function is perhaps best exemplified by high school social groups, which are often characterized at least in part by the groups' favorite music—pop junkies versus indie fans and metalheads. A song popular during a particular year can seem emblematic of that time, and the people and circumstances associated with it. Familiarity with church hymns defines one kind of community; familiarity with protest songs defines another. People list their favorite bands on online dating profiles as a way to communicate who they are. Musical knowledge and preferences bear traces not only of our individual characteristics, but also of the communities and moments that have shaped us.

Chapter 8
The future

From its disparate roots in diverse fields, the psychology of music has coalesced into a cohesive research area. Yet some of music's most compelling mysteries remain elusive. Consider a question such as, what makes a good performance? The psychology of music cannot answer it. This state of affairs could be viewed as an indictment of the field, a sketch of its future potential, or an intimation that the question might benefit from being asked a different way. If what counted as an answer were a universally applicable formula connecting judgments of quality with specific acoustic manipulations, then existing work in the psychology of music can be understood to have conclusively demonstrated that the question is unanswerable. Even within relatively narrow communities—such as the community of expert performers of Western classical piano music—significant disagreement exists about which performances are best. Without a universally applicable standard for "good," no formula can connect acoustic patterns with quality; rather, the background and circumstances of the listener and the culture within which the performance is happening must be considered, pushing the question into more intriguing but challenging territory.

Work in the psychology of music has already mapped some of the contours of this landscape. It has demonstrated, for example, that a performance's perceived quality cannot be assessed from the sound alone, given the fundamental contribution from information in the visual channel to the way music is heard and judged and the powerful impact of the context within which the sound is presented. Each time the psychology of music studies some aspect of musical experience, tries, and fails to account fully for some response (such as judgments of quality), it defines the topography of the problem a little more clearly. In this way, the psychology of music can continue to explore the limits of the aspects of human musical experience that are addressable by empirical methods. By running up against the borders of science, it can define new questions that would have been impossible to formulate without the attempt and failure of an experimental project. Humanistic and scientific approaches to music can proceed hand in hand, provoking each other into deeper insight than either would have been able to achieve alone.

Music and big data

The power of big data has become apparent in areas as diverse as forecasting the spread of infectious disease and predicting shopper behavior. Data relevant to music psychology—in the form, for example, of notes written, notes played, and hours listened—have always existed but have only recently been encoded in ways that make them amenable to easy large-scale analysis. If a researcher fifty years ago wanted to find out how far into a melody the first large leap tends to occur, the project would have required an impractically time-consuming period of pen-and-paper tallying: paging through each score, eyeballing the leap, and counting the beats preceding it. Today, that same researcher has access to digital search-and-manipulation toolkits that can probe vast databases of scores and performances to answer the same question in less than a minute.

Corpus studies harness the power of digital tools to identify patterns in large repertoires of music. How do recordings of European violinists from the 1960s differ from recordings of

American violinists from the 1960s? What stylistic features distinguished East Coast hip hop from West Coast hip hop in the 1990s? Digital tools can dispatch with these questions quickly, providing specific, provocative insights that—in partnership with broad humanistic inquiry—can propel richer accounts of the relationship between these styles and the cultures within which they developed.

Unlike most behavioral research, corpus studies do not require participants. Instead of measuring the responses of some sample of people recruited for a study, they analyze information that already exists—for example, notes people have previously written and played—to understand something about the cognitive processes that shaped them. But results from corpus studies can inspire new experiments that do use human participants. For example, corpus studies might identify the characteristics most common to genres like country or rock or pop. To understand perceptions of genre, subsequent experiments could then manipulate songs to add or remove these features, asking participants to classify the altered excerpts by genre. In scenarios like these, corpus studies and behavioral research partner with one another to illuminate broad topics, such as the perception of musical style.

Certain features that corpus studies reveal as typical—the most common distance between the bottom two voices in a musical texture versus the most common distance between the top two, to take one example—can be understood to stem from basic perceptual principles, such as the ear's differing ability to resolve pitch intervals at low and high frequencies. Others can be seen to vary from style to style as cultural influences change. Corpus studies have been particularly successful at addressing the question of how styles develop—how music written in Vienna in the 1880s sounds different from music written in Vienna in the 1850s or 1810s.

Corpus studies can trace the emergence and disappearance of compositional fads across time, such as the onset, peak, and decline of Auto-Tune in pop music or the onset, peak, and decline of the use of diminished seventh chords in Western classical music. By pairing statistics about diminished seventh chord usages per year with contemporary accounts of their perceived expressive quality, an arc can be identified. When the diminished seventh chord was rare, it was also expressively powerful— conveying an impression of mystery or danger. But as composers took advantage of its emotional sway, using it more and more, some of its expressive luster paled, rendering it less and less effective and ultimately something of a cliché. The statistical and receptive history of the diminished seventh chord supports the notion that expectancy violation contributes to musical expressivity. These chords tended to grip listeners more effectively when they were rare, relinquishing their expressive power as they became more common.

But notes written or recorded long ago are not the only type of big data relevant to music psychology. Perhaps the most tantalizing set of data would be a detailed account of the daily usage, context, and responses to music of large swaths of the population. Until recently, this seemed largely impossible to achieve. Now, however, about 75 percent of the world's population uses a mobile phone, and an increasing number of those phones function as music players as well, streaming music using services such as Spotify, Pandora, and Apple Music. These phones also often carry GPS trackers, which, overlaid with rich information from digital maps, can record whether people are listening at home, in a gym, or on a walk (and if so, at what pace). They can also record the time of day people are listening and what other apps they are using concurrently.

As if this were not enough, phones are also beginning to employ a host of physiological sensors, starting with heartbeat monitors but likely extending ultimately to a wide variety of instruments providing continuous measurements of phenomena like galvanic skin response (the sweat gland activation that occurs during emotional arousal) and respiration rate. It is easy to imagine a future in which information is available about what music vast numbers of people listen to when and where, along with information about their associated behavior and emotional response. This huge pool of data could enable music psychologists to answer questions about music, engagement, and context that are challenging to address in a laboratory setting, where listening experiences occur in isolation from so many of their embedded, real-world associations. But like other investigations of this scale, it raises critical issues about privacy, interpretation, and fairness. The history of the psychology of music demonstrates that pitfalls of this sort abound.

Data collected from phones could also provide the sort of longitudinal evidence that has previously been too expensive and painstaking to obtain. Previously, scientists who wanted to understand how musical tastes or abilities change across long timespans had to enroll large numbers of participants and entice them with monetary rewards to keep returning to the laboratory year in and year out. Despite incentives, studies like these suffer from high dropout rates. But if all participants need to do is carry around their phone and agree to allow some of its information to be sent to researchers, multiyear studies become much more feasible.

As if these aims were not grandiose enough, scientists and engineers at Google are attempting to harness the power of big data to create compelling machine-generated music. Their project, called Magenta, harnesses machine intelligence to analyze existing music and use the resulting insights to produce new compositions of its own, with an eye toward passing a musical version of the Turing test. The original Turing test proposed that the ultimate test of a machine's ability to think would be whether it could pass itself off as human in a typed conversational exchange. Google aims to see instead whether a machine might one day be able to pass itself off as human by writing a song.

Magenta's progress can be traced online, and while there is no mistaking it for Jimi Hendrix today, it is likely that its performance will vastly improve in the coming years.

Inventor Gil Weinberg has used similar machine intelligence strategies to build musician robots at Georgia Tech. He used statistical analyses of Thelonious Monk performances to train Shimon, a robot marimba player, to listen to a human musical partner and provide convincing improvised responses. Separately, he built a prosthetic, stick-wielding third arm drummers can wear to augment their performance with improvisations that continually adapt to the music in the room. In effect, this device allows musicians to experience a sense of cyborg performance, where they control some of what is happening, but the prosthetic arm controls the rest. Since many musicians describe a kind of embodied knowledge where their hands at times seem to "know" more than their heads—times when their fingers fly toward a sequence of just-right notes that they did not have time to plan and conceptualize in explicit terms—the experience of ceding some of the control to the stick might seem eerily familiar.

10. Shimon, a marimba-playing robot designed by Gil Weinberg, can improvise jazz dialogues with human performers, listening to their contributions and creating musical responses on the spot.

Earworms and musical memory

Since 2000, a body of work has developed on the phenomenon of tunes that get stuck in your head. So-called earworms affect more than 90 percent of people at least once a week, and historical records show that they predate the onset of modern recording technology. However, since repeated and recent exposure to a song are two of the best earworm predictors, technology that enables frequent relistening has probably increased their prevalence.

Earworms tend to be composed of short melodic snippets that play again and again in people's heads, outside of volitional control. They serve as perhaps the best demonstration of the way that music can capture people, making them feel as if they are imaginatively participating, even when they are really just sitting at a desk, and even when there is really no music playing at all. In the coming years, psychologists will seek to build on recent work to understand what makes music so especially well-suited to triggering this circuitry, and what makes some music even better at it than others. (People consistently rate certain songs, like Carly Rae Jepsen's "Call Me Maybe" and Disney's "It's a Small World" as especially sticky).

Earworms also illuminate the mysterious workings of memory particularly well. They can be triggered in remarkably oblique ways; for example, glimpsing a poster of someone who looks vaguely likely the fictional Gaston can trigger an intense bout of "No one *fights* like Gaston" half an hour later. Noticing that it is a particularly happy afternoon can elicit unbidden mental replays of tunes by Pharrell.

Similarly astonishing is the way that the entire course of songs that have gone unheard for decades can come rushing back in vivid detail when mentioned. How is it possible to have been storing all that music all that time without even remembering it was there? These feats of musical memory can serve as a useful vehicle for other types of information, as college students are often pleased to discover when they realize they can still list all the countries of the world thanks to childhood exposure to the Animaniacs song. Marketing companies exploit this capacity all the time, hitching a desired message to a catchy melodic wagon ("Gimme a break...").

These effects depend on music's tendency to be stored as a sequence, with one event following another in prescribed order within individual groupings, such as a phrase. People can often only access memory for the later part of a musical passage by starting at the beginning of a group. Once they have started remembering it, they often cannot stop until they get to the end of a group. For example, if I want to think about the note on which the word "fall" is sung in "Ring Around the Rosie," I have to start at "we all" in order to get to "fall," and then I have a hard time resisting continuing to "down."

Despite that speech is also made up of acoustic events following one another in time, people do not remember it in the same way. Asked to recap a conversation, people tend to provide a summary that captures the basic content of what was said without replicating the particular words. Asked to recall a song, however, people tend to sing the actual tune, note for note—in fact, it is hard to imagine what a musical summary might look or sound like. Musical memory tends to be quite faithful in nature—people asked to imagine a song tend to do so at roughly the correct pitch and tempo. Work in music psychology in coming years will likely harness the increasing power of neuroscience to understand the circuitry that underlies musical memory in greater detail.

Cross-cultural approaches

Psychological research typically relies on studying small samples of people intended to be representative of a general population. Researchers use statistics to assess the likelihood that effects found within their sample would generalize to the larger group. But because of practical constraints, most participants in psychology studies are undergraduates at universities in the West. Yet results from these studies are often taken to represent human cognition broadly construed.

In addition to relying disproportionately on Western university students as participants, music psychology tends to rely disproportionately on Western classical music as stimuli. Not only might the field be accused of generalizing from a subset of people with specific cultural experiences in order to understand human music cognition, but also of generalizing from a small slice of the world's music.

For the most part, these limitations did not arise out of willful negligence on the part of the research community. Rather, a series of social and systemic factors conspired to push research in this direction. First, many music psychologists grew up as classical musicians—there is a particularly well-worn path from classical guitar and piano into the hallways of music academe. Interdisciplinary work like music psychology requires its practitioners to master multiple fields, so with expertise in the Western system already under the belt, many scholars set off to integrate this knowledge with the tools and techniques of cognitive science rather than learn about new musical domains.

Existing divisions in music scholarship have not helped the situation. The study of non-Western music tends to be undertaken within the context of a discipline called ethnomusicology, with its own conferences, journals, and programs that sometimes regrettably run in parallel to those of musicology. Ethnomusicologists, committed to understanding music as a product of human culture, are not always enamored of the discipline of psychology, which they can view as insufficiently alert to the culturally constructed nature of its tools and methodologies.

Music psychologists generally look to cross-cultural work to help illuminate the human mind, but ethnomusicologists tend to view the mind as a product of human culture, rendering cross-cultural comparisons problematic. Cross-cultural work requires lots of time and funding for travel as well as expertise in multiple languages and musical systems and in the various disciplines of cognitive science. Because the people with expertise on the music side and the people with expertise on the psychology side tend to differ foundationally on the susceptibility of the human mind to particular types of study, it is difficult to put together effective collaborative teams for these sorts of projects. Even when the teams are capable of being assembled, research that falls between the cracks of established disciplines can be difficult to fund, with agencies devoted to one perspective or the other finding the proposal insufficiently representative of or central to their field. Nevertheless, as the imperative of transcending disciplinary boundaries to address big questions becomes more widely recognized, this research is starting to find a way.

Successful cross-cultural work devises tasks that do not rely on verbalization, allowing experiments to work even in places where no word that precisely translates to "music" exists. Nori Jacoby and colleagues used a musical game of telephone to reveal rhythmic biases in American and Tsimané listeners in a remote region of Bolivia. Participants in the study listened to a randomly generated rhythm and tapped it back. This tapping response was recorded and replayed. Again, participants were asked to tap it back. Across multiple iterations of listening and tapping, the rhythms people produced tended to reflect their basic expectations about how sounds typically go. For both American and Tsimané listeners, this meant converging on rhythms composed of simple integer ratios. Intriguingly, although listeners from both cultures settled on simple integer ratios, the particular ratios favored by the two groups differed systematically. American listeners produced ratios that are commonly found in Western music, and Tsimané listeners produced ratios commonly found in their music.

This study identified a shared bias toward simple integer ratios—particularly to the ratios typically heard in the surrounding musical culture—for two groups of people whose music has developed independently. The impact of the surrounding soundscape on rhythmic preferences has been established in cultures with less mutual independence as well. When asked to choose from different rhythmic groupings of individual tones, native Japanese speakers prefer long-short groupings, while native English speakers prefer short-long ones, mirroring a rhythmic distinction in the two languages. Although people probably could not verbally identify the ratios typically heard in their music or language, designs such as these can provide implicit evidence for the ability, making them a powerful tool for studying cognition across cultural boundaries.

Bridges among science, humanities, and the arts

The psychology of music occupies an intriguing nexus among the arts, the humanities, and the sciences. Since the 1980s, it has been bringing people with expertise in each of these areas together to exchange ideas, collaborate, and plan research. In many ways, it has been on the intellectual vanguard, making interdisciplinary progress happen before the value of reaching across specialty domains was widely recognized in academia.

Yet the potential for discovery and dialogue is even greater. Scientific findings make their way into the popular press with alacrity, but work in the humanities, which often resists easy encapsulation, is often slower to translate into the public sphere. To make things more uneven, science—and particularly neuroscience—can be seen to possess an authority not always extended to other intellectual undertakings.

The systemic asymmetry between the reception of science and the humanities affects music psychology's capacity to thrive. With traditional incentives often disproportionately rewarding scientific studies that make easy claims about musicality over the more nuanced and careful accounts that reflect rigorous humanistic input, a danger exists that the field's increasingly sophisticated tools will be marshalled to support prevailing assumptions rather than drive theoretical discovery.

One of the most dazzling of these new tools takes research out of the cramped basement laboratory and into real-world performance spaces. Several research institutes around the world have outfitted special concert halls with motion capture, EEG, and physiological sensors, placing audience response tablets at each seat and installing technology that can manipulate the acoustic characteristics of the space. Facilities like these make it much easier for listeners to have the kind of musical experience psychologists want to study. Hearing music played by live performers in a darkened hall can be a riveting event not easily approximated by listening over headphones in a soundproof booth under fluorescent lighting.

An audience at a classical concert typically does not provide much behavioral evidence of their feelings, judgments, and responses. People undergoing a profound, transformative listening experience sit silently much the same as people formulating their grocery list in their head. By providing a venue to subtly measure everything that is measurable, from palm sweat to torso sways to neural activity, these wired concert halls provide a tantalizing chance for illuminating the hidden aspects of musical processing.

But to harness the promise of these facilities, researchers must develop questions and theories that reflect sustained thoughtfulness about music and musical behavior. Diverse voices with expertise in musical practices from around the world must come together to formulate them. Firsthand accounts of music's power must be listened to and woven into the research design, so that emotional experiences are categorized not merely as happy or sad and evaluations extend beyond liked or disliked. Performer expertise about the inner workings of musical expressivity must be allowed to shape experiments on timing and perception. Researchers must move fluidly back and forth between rich descriptive characterizations of musical behaviors and the rigorous, controlled designs necessary for studying them.

In fact, this capacity for interplay and flexible thinking seems ever more critical to the broad challenges of the twenty-first century, beyond the specifics of the psychology of music. By providing a laboratory for thinking between the sciences and the humanities, music psychology can fuel innovation that transcends its own disciplinary borders, while helping us understand a fundamental human attribute—musicality—that is key to our identity, our eccentricity, and our ability to understand one another.

References

Chapter 1

The *Scientific American*'s take on Seashore's test can be found in Harold Cary, "Are You a Musician?" *Scientific American* (December 1922), 376–377.

The study that inspired the notion of a Mozart effect is Frances H. Rauscher, Gordon L. Shaw, and Catherine N. Ky, "Music and Spatial Task Performance," *Nature* 365 (1993): 611.

Jeanne Bamberger's work on the development of music perception can be found in Jeanne Bamberger, *The Mind behind the Musical Ear: How Children Develop Musical Intelligence* (Cambridge, MA: Harvard University Press, 1991).

Chapter 2

The overview of the Blackfoot term *saapup* comes from Bruno Nettl, "An Ethnomusicologist Contemplates Universals in Musical Sound and Musical Culture," in *The Origins of Music*, edited by Nils L. Wallin, Björn Merker, and Steven Brown, 463–472 (Cambridge, MA: MIT Press, 2000).

The discovery that the Tsimane' did not find consonance more pleasant than dissonance is reported in Josh H. McDermott, Alan F. Schulz, Eduardo A. Undurruga, and Ricardo A. Godoy, "Indifference to Dissonance in Native Amazonians Reveals Cultural Variation in Music Perception," *Nature* 535 (2016): 547–550.

The account of floating intentionality comes from Ian Cross, "Is Music the Most Important Thing We Ever Did? Music, Development, and Evolution," in *Music, Mind and Science*, edited by Suk Won Yi, 10–39 (Seoul: Seoul National University Press, 1999).

Martin Clayton's taxonomy of musical functions is listed in Martin Clayton, "The Social and Personal Functions of Music in Cross-Cultural Perspective," in *The Oxford Handbook of Music Psychology*, edited by Susan Hallam, Ian Cross, and Michael Thaut, 35–43 (Oxford: Oxford University Press, 2009).

Research about the corpus callosum in musicians is reported in Gottfried Schlaug, Lutz Jäncke, Yanxiong Huang, Jochen F. Staiger, and Helmuth Steinmetz, "Increased Corpus Callosum Size in Musicians," *Neuropsychologia* 33.8 (1995): 1047–1055.

The effect of musical training on pitch tracking in the brainstem is detailed in Patrick C. M. Wong, Erika Skoe, Nicole M. Russo, Tasha Dees, and Nina Kraus, "Musical Experience Shapes Human Brainstem Encoding of Linguistic Pitch Patterns," *Nature Neuroscience* 10.4 (2007): 420–422.

The study identifying the role of the reward network in music listening is Anne J. Blood and Robert J. Zatorre, "Intensely Pleasurable Responses to Music Correlate with Activity in Brain Regions Implicated in Reward and Emotion," *Proceedings of the National Academy of Sciences of the United States of America* 98.20 (2001): 11818–11823.

The relationship between music and gait in Parkinson's disease is outlined in Gerald C. McIntosh, Susan H. Brown, Ruth R. Rice, and Michael Thaut, "Rhythmic Auditory-Motor Facilitation of Gait Patterns in Patients with Parkinson's Disease," *Journal of Neurology, Neurosurgery & Psychiatry* 62.1 (1997): 22–26.

The effect of melodic intonation therapy on aphasia is chronicled in Pascal Belin, Ph. van Eeckhout, M. Zilbovicius, Ph. Remy, C. François, S. Guillaume, F. Chain, G. Rancurel, and Y. Samson, "Recovery from Nonfluent Aphasia after Melodic Intonation Therapy: A PET Study," *Neurology* 47.6 (1996): 1504–1511.

Research on music and premature infants is summarized in Jayne Standley, "Music Therapy Research in the NICU: An Updated Meta-analysis," *Neonatal Network* 31.5 (2012): 311–316.

Research about Snowball's capacity to entrain can be found in Aniruddh D. Patel, John R. Iversen, Micah R. Bregman, and Irena Schulz, "Experimental Evidence for Synchronization to a Musical

Beat in a Nonhuman Animal," *Current Biology* 19.10 (2009): 827–830.

The finding about goldfish sorting music by composer comes from Kazutaka Shinozuka, Haruka Ono, and Shigeru Watanabe, "Reinforcing and Discriminative Stimulus Properties of Music in Goldfish," *Behavioural Processes* 99 (2013): 26–33.

The paper about carp and musical style is Ava R. Chase, "Musical Discriminations by Carp," *Animal Learning & Behavior* 29.4 (2001): 336–353.

Information about melody learning in the bullfinch comes from Jürgen Nicolai, Christina Gundacker, Katharina Teeselink, and Hans Rudolf Güttinger, "Human Melody Singing by Bullfinches Gives Hints about a Cognitive Note Sequence Processing," *Animal Cognition* 17.1 (2014): 143–155.

Chapter 3

David Huron discusses wrong note melodies in *Sweet Anticipation: Music and the Psychology of Expectation* (Cambridge, MA: MIT Press, 2006).

The finding about overlaps between musical and linguistic syntax processing comes from L. Robert Slevc, Jason C. Rosenberg, and Aniruddh D. Patel, "Making Psycholinguistics Musical: Self-Paced Reading Time Evidence for Shared Processing of Linguistic and Musical Syntax," *Psychonomic Bulletin & Review* 16.2 (2009): 374–381.

The classic paper on statistical learning for musical tones is Jenny R. Saffran, Elizabeth K. Johnson, Richard N. Aslin, and Elissa L. Newport. "Statistical Learning of Tone Sequences by Human Infants and Adults," *Cognition* 70.1 (1999): 27–52.

Deryck Cooke's quixotic attempt to analyze musical meanings can be found in his *The Language of Music* (New York: Oxford University Press, 1959).

The account of consensus in narrative descriptions of music can be found in Elizabeth Hellmuth Margulis, "An Exploratory Study of Narrative Responses to Music," *Music Perception* 35 (2017): 235–248.

The research on bimusicality can be found in Patrick C. M. Wong, Anil K. Roy, and Elizabeth Hellmuth Margulis, "Bimusicalism: The

Implicit Dual Enculturation of Cognitive and Affective Systems," *Music Perception* 27 (2009): 81–88.

The speech-to-song illusion is presented in Diana Deutsch, Trevor Henthorn, and Rachael Lapidis, "Illusory Transformation from Speech to Song," *Journal of the Acoustical Society of America* 129.4 (2011): 2245–2252.

Chapter 4

The research on musical groove comes from Petr Janata, Stefan T. Tomic, and Jason Haberman, "Sensorimotor Coupling in Music and the Psychology of the Groove," *Journal of Experimental Psychology: General* 141.1 (2012): 54–75.

The findings on auditory scene analysis are covered in Albert S. Bregman, *Auditory Scene Analysis: The Perceptual Organization of Sound* (Cambridge, MA: MIT Press, 1994).

The study about failures in large-scale form perception is Nicholas Cook, "The Perception of Large-Scale Tonal Closure," *Music Perception* 5.2 (1987): 197–205.

The study in which listeners were able to tell roughly where in a piece various segments had come from is Eric F. Clarke and Carol L. Krumhansl, "Perceiving Musical Time," *Music Perception* 7.3 (1990): 213–252.

The book in which a philosopher advocates for the primacy of small-scale over large-scale listening is Jerrold Levinson, *Music in the Moment* (Ithaca, NY: Cornell University Press, 1998).

The study that demonstrated that babies could translate bouncing patterns to auditory ones is Jessica Phillips-Silver and Laurel Trainor, "Feeling the Beat: Movement Influences Infant Rhythm Perception," *Science* 308 (2005): 1430.

Research comparing rhythmic patterns in French and English music can be found in Anirrudh R. Patel and Joseph R. Daniele, "An Empirical Comparison of Rhythm in Language and Music," *Cognition* 87.1 (2003): B35–B45.

Chapter 5

The comparison of timing profiles for different pianists can be found in a pair of reports: Bruno H. Repp, "Diversity and Commonality in Music Performance: An Analysis of Timing Microstructure in

Schumann's Träumerei," *Haskins Laboratories Status Report on Speech Research* SR-111 (1992): 227–260; and Bruno H. Repp, "Expressive Timing in Schumann's Träumerei": An Analysis of Performances by Graduate Student Pianists," *Haskins Laboratories Status Report on Speech Research* SR-117/118 (1994): 141–160.

Information about the relative contribution of expressive timing and dynamics to listener preferences for performances comes from Bruno H. Repp, "A Microcosm of Musical Expression: III. Contributions of Timing and Dynamics to the Aesthetic Impressions of Pianists' Performances of the Initial Measures of Chopin's Etude in E Major," *Journal of the Acoustical Society of America* 106.1 (1999): 469–479.

Research about the impact of facial expressions on perceived dissonance is reported in William F. Thompson, Phil Graham, and Frank A. Russo, "Seeing Music Performance: Visual Influences on Perception and Experience," *Semiotica* 156.1–4 (2005): 203–227.

Motion capture studies of perceived expressivity in violin performances are detailed in Jane W. Davidson, *The Perception of Expressive Movement in Music Performance* (PhD diss., City University of London, 1991).

Research about the effect of information about the performer's level of professionalism on performance ratings comes from two sources: Carolyn A. Kroger and Elizabeth Hellmuth Margulis, "But They Told Me It Was Professional": Extrinsic Factors in the Evaluation of Musical Performance," *Psychology of Music* 45.1 (2017): 49–64; and Gökhan Aydogan, Nicole Flaig, Srekar N. Ravi, Edward W. Large, Samuel M. McClure, and Elizabeth Hellmuth Margulis, "Overcoming Bias: Cognitive Control Reduces Susceptibility to Framing Effects in Evaluating Musical Performance," *Scientific Reports* 8 (2018): 6229.

The study demonstrating that violinists rated most highly had engaged in more deliberate practice than other violinists is K. Anders Ericsson, Ralf Th. Krampe, and Clemens Tesch-Romer, "The Role of Deliberate Practice in the Acquisition of Expert Performance," *Psychological Review* 100.3 (1993): 363–406.

Research supporting the role of genes in music ability can be found in Miriam A. Mosing, Guy Madison, Nancy L. Pedersen, Ralf Kuja-Halkola, and Fredrik Ullén, "Practice Does Not Make Perfect: No Causal Effect of Music Practice on Music Ability," *Psychological Science* 25 (2014): 1795–1803.

The neuroimaging study of jazz performers discussed in the chapter is Charles J. Limb and Allen R. Braun, "Neural Substrates of Spontaneous Musical Performance: An fMRI Study of Jazz Improvisation," *PLoS ONE* 3.2 (2008): e1679.

Chapter 6

Multiple metaphorical pitch mappings are listed in Zohar Eitan and Renee Timmers, "Beethoven's Last Piano Sonata and Those Who Follow Crocodiles: Cross-Domain Mappings of Auditory Pitch in a Musical Context," *Cognition* 114.3 (2010): 405–422.

The original probe tone study is reported in Carol L. Krumhansl and Roger N. Shepard, "Quantification of the Hierarchy of Tonal Functions within a Diatonic Context," *Journal of Experimental Psychology: Human Perception and Performance* 5.4 (1979): 579–594.

The finding that infants listen longer to music with pauses in their typical locations is reported in Carol L. Krumhansl and Peter W. Jusczyk, "Infants' Perception of Phrase Structure in Music," *Psychological Science* 1 (1990): 70–73.

Responses to Western and Javanese scales are chronicled in Laurel J. Trainor and Sandra E. Trehub, "A Comparison of Infants' and Adults' Sensitivity to Western Musical Structure," *Journal of Experimental Psychology: Human Perception and Performance* 18.2 (1992): 394–402.

The research about perceptions of isochronous and nonisochronous meters is reported in Erin E. Hannon and Sandra E. Trehub, "Tuning in to Musical Rhythms: Infants Learn More Readily than Adults," *Proceedings of the National Academy of Sciences* 102.35 (2005): 12639–12643.

The study demonstrating that children's synchronization abilities improve in social contexts is Sebastian Kirschner and Michael Tomasello, "Joint Drumming: Social Context Facilitates Synchronization in Preschool Children," *Journal of Experimental Child Psychology* 102.3 (2009): 299–314.

The Absorption in Music Scale comes from Gillian M. Sandstrom and Frank A. Russo, "Absorption in Music: Development of a Scale to Identify Individuals with Strong Emotional Responses to Music," *Psychology of Music* 41.2 (2013): 216–228.

The Gold MSI is detailed in Daniel Müllensiefen, Bruno Gingras, Jason Musil, and Lauren Stewart, "The Musicality of Non-musicians: An Index for Assessing Musical Sophistication in the General Population," *PLoS ONE* 9.6 (2014): e101091.

Chapter 7

A list of hypothesized mechanisms through which music evokes emotion can be found in Patrik N. Juslin and Daniel Västfjäll, "Emotional Responses to Music: The Need to Consider Underlying Mechanisms," *Behavioral and Brain Sciences* 31 (2008): 559–621.

Petr Janata's work on music and autobiographical memory can be found in Petr Janata, "The Neural Architecture of Music-Evoked Autobiographical Memories," *Cerebral Cortex* 19.11 (2009): 2579–2594.

The link between surprise and musical affect is described in Leonard B. Meyer, *Emotion and Meaning in Music* (Chicago: University of Chicago Press, 1956).

Research on the inverted-U preference curve can be found in Karl K. Szpunar, E. Glenn Schellenberg, and Patricia Pliner, "Liking and Memory for Musical Stimuli as a Function of Exposure," *Journal of Experimental Psychology: Learning, Memory and Cognition* 30.2 (2004): 370–381.

Alf Gabrielsson's work on peak experiences of music is summarized in Alf Gabrielsson, *Strong Experiences with Music: Music Is Much More than Just Music*, translated by Rod Bradbury (New York: Oxford University Press, 2011).

Chapter 8

The study about rhythmic biases in American and Tsimane' listeners is Nori Jacoby and Josh H. McDermott, "Integer Ratio Priors on Musical Rhythm Revealed Cross-Culturally by Iterated Reproduction," *Current Biology* 27.3 (2017): 359–370.

Further reading

Ashley, Richard, and Renee Timmers, eds. *The Routledge Companion to Music Cognition*. Abingdon, UK: Routledge, 2017.

Hallam, Susan, Ian Cross, and Michael Thaut, eds. *The Oxford Handbook of Music Psychology*. Oxford: Oxford University Press, 2016.

Hargreaves, David, and Adrian North. *The Social Psychology of Music*. New York: Oxford University Press, 1997.

Honing, Henkjan. *The Origins of Musicality*. Cambridge, MA: MIT Press, 2018.

Huron, David. *Sweet Anticipation: Music and the Psychology of Expectation*. Cambridge, MA: MIT Press, 2006.

Huron, David. *Voice Leading: The Science behind a Musical Art*. Cambridge, MA: MIT Press, 2016.

Jourdain, Robert. *Music, the Brain, and Ecstasy: How Music Captures Our Imagination*. New York: William Morrow, 2008.

Koelsch, Stefan. *Music and Brain*. New York: Wiley-Blackwell, 2012.

Lehmann, Andreas C., John A. Sloboda, and Robert H. Woody. *Psychology for Musicians: Understanding and Acquiring the Skills*. New York: Oxford University Press, 2007.

Levitin, Daniel J. *This Is Your Brain on Music: The Science of a Human Obsession*. New York: Plume/Penguin, 2007.

London, Justin. *Hearing in Time: Psychological Aspects of Musical Meter*. New York: Oxford University Press, 2012.

Mannes, Elena. *The Power of Music: Pioneering Discoveries in the New Science of Song*. New York: Walker, 2011.

Margulis, Elizabeth Hellmuth. *On Repeat: How Music Plays the Mind*. New York: Oxford University Press, 2014.

Mithen, Steven. *The Singing Neanderthals: The Origins of Music, Language, Mind, and Body*. Cambridge, MA: Harvard University Press, 2007.

Patel, Aniruddh D. *Music and the Brain*. Chantilly, VA: The Great Courses, 2016.

Patel, Aniruddh D. *Music, Language, and the Brain*. New York: Oxford University Press, 2007.

Powell, John. *Why You Love Music: From Mozart to Metallica—The Emotional Power of Beautiful Sounds*. New York: Little, Brown, 2016.

Sacks, Oliver. *Musicophilia: Tales of Music and the Brain*. New York: Knopf, 2007.

Sloboda, John. *Exploring the Musical Mind: Cognition, Emotion, Ability, Function*. New York: Oxford University Press, 2005.

Tan, Siu-Lan, Annabel J. Cohen, Scott D. Lipscomb, and Roger A. Kendall, eds. *The Psychology of Music in Multimedia*. New York: Oxford University Press, 2013.

Tan, Siu-Lan, Peter Pfordresher, and Rom Harré. *Psychology of Music: From Sound to Significance*. New York: Psychology Press, 2010.

Thaut, Michael H. *Rhythm, Music, and the Brain: Scientific Foundations and Clinical Applications*. Abingdon, UK: Routledge, 2005.

Thaut, Michael H., and Volker Hoemberg, eds. *Handbook of Neurologic Music Therapy*. New York: Oxford University Press, 2014.

Thompson, William F. *Music, Thought, and Feeling: Understanding the Psychology of Music*. New York: Oxford University Press, 2014.

Index

A

absolute pitch, 81–82, 91, 92
Absorption in Music Scale (AIMS), 90
acoustics, 120
action, 60–62
addiction, 103
adolescence, 98, 99, 105
advertising, 42
aesthetics, 21, 31, 56, 66, 69, 102–103, 107
AIMS. *See* Absorption in Music Scale
alliteration, 48
amusia, 93–94
anhedonia, 94
animals, 29–31
anticipation, 38, 51, 52, 102
anxiety, 76
aphasia, 18, 93
articulation, 63–64, 69
audience, 120
auditory cortex, 24, 25, 94
auditory imagination, 58
auditory-motor link, 30, 61, 76, 107
autism, 92–93
autobiographical memory, 98

B

babies. *See* infants
Bach, Johann Sebastian, 11, 31, 56, 57, 65
Bacon, Francis, 4
balance, 27
Balkan music, 68
Bamberger, Jeanne, 18
basal ganglia, 25, 27, 61
basilar membrane, 55
beats, 11, 12, 21, 43, 49–53, 60, 61, 86
Beethoven, Ludwig Van, 9, 58, 106
behavioral research, 2, 13–16
beta blockers, 76
bias, 72, 119
big data, 110–114
birds, 29–31
blood pressure, 28–29
bodily movement, 50–51, 60–62, 86
bonding, 32, 52, 62, 107, 108
brain, 23–27, 28, 37, 38, 61, 72, 75–76, 77, 98–99, 103.
    See also *specific parts*
  damage, 18
  stem, 44, 45, 97
  structure, 32–33
Bregman, Albert, 54, 55

C

cerebellum, 61
children, 8, 10, 14, 19, 22, 24, 28, 86–87, 88–89, 91–92
chills, 25, 100–101
Chomsky, Noam, 39
Chopin, Frédéric, *67*
chords, 37, 112
cinematic associations, 41–42
classical music, 8–9, 58, 62, 105, 112
Clayton, Martin, 22
clinical approaches, 18
cochlea, *55*
cognitive fluency, 72
cognitive impairments, 28
cognitive neuroscience methods, 16–18
cognitive science, 2, 10, 34
Cohen, Leonard, 42
communication, 4, 21, 22, 34, 43, 66, 72, 107–108. *See also* language
community, 108
competitions, 70
complexity, 103–105, *104*
computer modeling, 11–12
concerts, 52, 72, 120
consonance, 20–21, 83–84
context, 87, 106
Cooke, Deryck, 41
coordination, 23, 27, 34
corpus callosum, 23, 24
corpus studies, 12–13, 110–112
cortex, *55*, 61
creativity, 76–78
Cross, Ian, 21
cross-cultural approaches, 116–121
Csikszentmihalyi, Mihaly, 77
culture, 1, 2, 5–6, 9, 12–14, 20–21, 33, 43, 63, 117, 119

D

dance, 20, 25, 50–51, 60, 86, 105
data, 110–114

Davidson, Jane, 71
dementia, 18, 28, 98
Deutsch, Diana, 47
Deutscher, Alma, 91
developmental psychology, 18
digitization, 12
diminished chords, 112
dissonance, 20–21, 84
dopamine, 25–26
dorsolateral prefrontal cortex, 77
duple meter, 49, 50, 61
dynamics, 48, 49, 63–65, 66, 69
dyslexia, 45

E

eardrums, 24, 55
ears, 54, 71
earworms, 115–116
eccentricity, 121
ecological validity, 13
EEG, 16–17, *17*, 37, 41, 60, 120
electronic dance music, 25
emotional response, 90, 95, 96–102, *97*, 112–113
emotions, 4, 5, 15, 19, 23, 25, 42, 68, 71, 72, 86–87, 88, 91–92, 107, 108
empirical methodology, *15*
engagement, 25, 38, 43, 45, 48, 89, 107, 113
enjoyment, 72–73, 103–106, *104*
errors, 38, 73
ethnomusicology, 117–118
evaluative conditioning, 98, 100
everyday listening, *35*
everyday music, 6
evolutionary origins, of music, 32–33
exaptation, 33
expectations, 67
experience, 2, 4, 15, 43, 48, 68–73, 95–96, 101–102, 105
expressivity, 63–68, *67*, 69, 71, 75, 100, 112, 121

extroverts, 105
eye-tracking studies, 74

F

facial expressions, 71, 87, 94, 99
familiarity, 103–106, *104*
fMRI, 16–17, 77, 103
formal instruction, 40, 87–91
frequency, 44, 45, 48, 55, *56*,
    79–80

G

Gabrielsson, Alf, 19, 101
gait, 27
Galilei, Vincenzo, 4
galvanic skin response, 112–113
genetics, 33, 75
genre, 31, 105, 108, 111
Gestalt psychology, 54, 55, 56
goals, 45, 75, 96
Goldsmiths Musical
    Sophistication Index
    (Gold-MSI), 90
Google, 11, 113
goosebumps. *See* chills
GPS trackers, 112
grammar, 26, 34–35
groove, 51
group identity, 108
group synchrony, 30
Guantánamo Bay, 29

H

habits, 25
Hannon, Erin, 84
"Happy Birthday," 53
harmony, 85–86
health, 18, 26–29
heartbeat, 25, 83, 112
heart rate, 69
Helmholtz, Hermann, 5
heuristics, 56

humanities, 10, 91, 119–121
Huron, David, 36
hymns, 41

I

identity, 21, 105, 107, 108, 121
imagination, 41–42, 43
imitation, 76
improvisation, 76–78, 91
Indian classical music, 43, 68
individual differences, 89–91
infants, 10, 14, 22, 28, 32,
    39–40, 61, 83–86. *See also*
    children
inferior frontal gyrus, 27
inner ear, 24
inner voice, 74
integer ratios, 3, 4, 59, 60,
    118–119
intelligence, 5, 8, 9, 14, 75, 88, 92
intensity, 100
inter-hand synchrony, 73
interpretation, 14, *15*
intervals, 21, 41, 70, 71, 83–84, 111
isochronous meter, 84–85
Iverson, John, 30

J

Jacboy, Nori, 118
Jackendoff, Ray, 39
Janata, Peter, 98
Javanese pelog scale, 84
jazz, 77, 105, 108

K

key, 35, 37, 74, *81*, 86, 95
King, B. B., 70–71
King, Martin Luther, Jr., 48
King Crimson, 105
Koelsch, Stefan, 41
Kraus, Nina, 89
Krumhansl, Carol, 80

L

language, 10, 20, 23, 26, 34–41, 54, 59–60, 85, 93, 119
language-music interactions, 43–45
learning, 38–41, 75–76
leitmotivs, 107–108
Lerdahl, Fred, 39
lessons, 87–89
Levinson, Jerrold, 58
Lewis-Clack, Rex, 92
liking, 103–106
linguistics, 10, 41, 59–60
listening, 22, 24, 26, 35, 43, 49, 59, 60–62, 68, 87, 96, 97, 101–102, 103–106, 104
Liszt, Franz, 42, 99
literacy, 23
looping, 47–48
loudness, 11, 12, 73, 87, 97
lullabies, 22, 87

M

machine-generated music, 113–114
machine learning, 11
Magenta, 11, 113–114
marketing, 116
Maslow, Abraham, 101
mathematics, 1, 3, 4, 20, 89, 92
mating calls, 30
Mbuti, 107
McGurk effect, 70
meaning, 36, 41–43
mechanics, of performance, 73–74
media, 117
Melodic Intonation Therapy, 27
melody, 23, 31, 45, 54–60, 68, 74, 82–83, 84, 93–94
memory, 26, 28, 43, 45, 48, 58, 73, 88, 94, 95, 98, 115–116
metal, 105
meter, 5, 49–53, 61, 62, 69, 84
Meyer, Leonard, 100
middle ear, 55

MIDI transcriptions, 31
mirror neurons, 99
misinterpretation, 14
mobile phones, 112–113
modality, 96
Montessori bells, 18
moods, 108
mother, 83
motivation, 75, 106–108
motor activation, 107
motor skills, 23, 91
motor system, 25, 43, 51, 61, 73, 93
movement, 22, 25, 86, 107
Mozart, Wolfgang Amadeus, 8–9, 11, 14, 85, 91
Müllensiefen, Daniel, 90
musical aptitude, 6–7, 7
musical experience, 2, 4, 48, 95–96
musical expressivity, 35–36
musical function, 106–108
musicality, 2–3, 18, 23, 30, 32, 79–83, 81, 83–87, 120
musical structures, 5, 21, 35, 47, 64–65, 69
music-language interactions, 43–45
music videos, 70–71

N

Nancarrow, Conlon, 52
narrative, 41–42
natural selection, 32–33
neonatal intensive care units (NICUs), 28
neural activity, 17, 75
neural circuitry, 23, 26–27, 38, 97–98
neuroaesthetics, 103
neuroimaging, 1, 16–18, 50–51, 77, 101, 103
neurons, 25, 99
neuroscience, 10, 16–18, 119
neurotransmitters, 25–26
NICUs. See neonatal intensive care units

nonisochronous meter, 84–85
nostalgia, 98, 99
notation, 10, 12, 34, 41, 59, 63
notes, 3, 21, 64, 73–74
numbers. *See* mathematics

O

orbitofrontal cortex, 25, 103
orchestras, 63, 100

P

pain tolerance, 28–29
Paravicini, Derek, 92
parents, 85, 105
Parkinson's disease, 27, 107
participatory music, 62, 93, 106
Patel, Aniruddh, 30
peak experiences, 101–102, 105
perception, 2, 3, 4, 24, 49–53, 54,
    59, 62, 79–83, *81*, 85, 88–89,
    111, 121
perceptual skills, 23
performance
    anxiety, 76
    cyborg, 114
    errors, 73
    experience of, 68–73
    expressivity in, 63–68, *67*, *69*,
        71, 75
    mechanics of, 73–74
    planning in, 73–74
    practice of, 74–76
    quality of, 109–110
performers, 63, 69
personality types, 88, 105
phonological awareness, 88–89
phrasing, 12, 69, 83
physics, 5, 16, 20
Pinker, Steven, 32
pitch, 21–23, 25, 64, 73, 86, 116.
    See also intervals; melody
    absolute, 81–82, 91, 92
    identification, 81–82

perception, 79–83, *81*
    processing, 93
    relative, 31, 81–82
    tracking, 44
planning, 73–74
plasticity, 85
Plato, 26
play, 21, 107
player piano, 52
pleasure, 25, 29, 51, 94, 100
pop music, 50, 105
practice, 74–76
preferences, 103–106, *104*
premotor cortex, 61, 99
prodigies, 91–93
program notes, 5
Prokofiev, Sergei, 35–36
pseudowords, 39–40
psychoacoustics, 54, 71
psycholinguistics, 34
Pythagoras, 3, 89

Q

qualitative approaches, 18–19

R

rap, 46
ratios. *See* integer ratios
reaction time, 13, 37
reading ability, 44–45, 89
recordings, 110–111, 115
reductionism, 5
rehabilitation, 107
Reich, Steve, 46
relative pitch, 31, 81–82
religion, 62
relistening, 101–102, 115
Remote Association Test, 76
repetition, 21, 22, 47–48, 101–102
Repp, Bruno, 65
resolution, 38
reward circuitry, 38, 72, 94, 103
rhyme, 46

Index

rhythm, 27, 44–45, 46, 49–53, 57, 59–61, 85, 118
rituals, 21
robots, 114

S

Saffran, Jenny, 39
savants, 91–93
scales, 21, 26, 31, 84, 86
scientific revolution, 4
Seashore, Carl, 6, 7, 14
semantic associations, 41–42
sexual selection, 32
Shimon (robot), 114, *114*
sight-reading, 74
Skinner, B. F., 10
Slevc, L. Robert, 37
Snowball, 30
social bonding, 32, 62, 107, 108
social skills, 23
special musical abilities, 91–93
special musical deficits, 93–94
spectograms, *46*
speech, 26, 27–28, 39, 43–44, 45–48, 69, 70, 73, 88–89
Star Wars, 108
Stravinsky, Igor, 30–31
subjective rhythmization, 50
superior temporal gyrus, 24
syllables, 39–40, 60, 70
synchrony, 62, 73, 86
syncopation, 50
syntax, 35–38

T

Telemann, Georg Philipp, 42
tempo, 51, 53, 64, *67*, 87, 116
temporal lobe, 24
tension, 38, 43, 100
theme songs, 82
therapeutic uses, of music, 18, 26–29, 107
timbre, 55, 56, 64, 66

time, 49–60, 62
timing, 63, 66, *67*, 68, 69, 84, 121
tonality, 80, 81
tone languages, 45
tone profile, *81*
tonoscope, 7
torso movement, 60
torture, 29
training, 24, 37, 43, 44–45, 73, 76, 87–89, 90
transcriptions, 31
tree structure analyses, 39
Trehub, Sandra, 84
triple meter, 49, 50, 61
Tsimané, 20–21, 84, 118
Turing test, 113

U

universality, 33, 84, 85, 109

V

ventral medial prefrontal cortex, 25
ventral striatum, 25
vibration, 3
videos, 70–71
visuals, 69–72, 99–100
visual skills, 23
Vivaldi, Antonio, 56
vocal learning, 29
vocal music, 41
voices, 54–60

W

Wagner, Richard, 107–108
Weinberg, Gil, 114, *114*
Williams, Andy, 29
Williams Syndrome, 18, 92–93
Wong, Patrick, 43
words, 35, 39–40, 41–42, 48
wrong notes, 35–36
Wundt, Wilhelm, 103–104
Wundt curve, 103, *104*

The Psychology of Music